GOD'S
INVITATION TO
Peace and Justice

SERMONS AND ESSAYS ON
SHALOM

Ronald J. Sider

JUDSON PRESS
PUBLISHERS SINCE 1824
VALLEY FORGE, PA

Judson Press has made every effort to trace the ownership of all quotes. In the event of a question arising from the use of a quote, we regret any error made and will be pleased to make the necessary correction in future printings and editions of this book.

Scripture quotations marked NIV are from the Holy Bible, New International Version®, NIV®. Copyright © 1973, 1978, 1984, 2011 by Biblical Inc.® Used by permission of Zondervan. All rights reserved worldwide. www.zondervan.com. The "NIV" and "New International Version" are trademarks registered in the United States Patent and Trademark Office by Biblica, Inc.®

Scripture quotations marked RSV are from the Revised Standard Version of the Bible, copyright 1946, 1952, and 1971 National Council of the Churches of Christ in the United States of America. Used by permission. All rights reserved.

Interior design by Wendy Ronga, Hampton Design Group.
Cover design by Danny Ellison.

Library of Congress Cataloging-in-Publication data
Names: Sider, Ronald J., author. Title: God's invitation to peace and justice: sermons and essays on Shalom/Ronald J. Sider. Description: Valley Forge, PA: Judson Press, 2021.
Identifiers: LCCN 2021011262 (print) | LCCN 2021011263 (ebook) | ISBN 9780817018276 (paperback) | ISBN 9780817082307 (epub) Subjects: LCSH: Christianity and justice—Miscellanea. | Social justice—Religious aspects—Christianity—Miscellanea. | Peace—Religious aspects—Christianity—Miscellanea. Classification: LCC BR115.J8 S575 2021 (print) | LCC BR115.J8 (ebook) | DDC 261.8—dc23
LC record available at https://lccn.loc.gov/2021011262
LC ebook record available at https://lccn.loc.gov/2021011263

Printed in the U.S.A.
First printing, 2021.

Contents

PART 1

Speeches and Essays

CHAPTER 1

An Evangelical Theology
of Liberation

This paper was originally presented on December 29, 1978, at the thirtieth annual meeting of the Evangelical Theological Society held at Trinity Evangelical Divinity School (Deerfield, Illinois) and later at a number of places, including Egypt, Australia, India, and Israel. It was later published in Kenneth S. Kantzer and Stanley N. Gundry, eds., *Perspectives on Evangelical Theology* (Grand Rapids: Baker, 1979), 117–33.

I hoped in 1978 for massive growth in evangelical understanding and living out of the biblical teaching about God's concern for the poor. In spite of the vast expansion of evangelical agencies working to combat global poverty, I do not think the evangelical world in North America has substantially understood or lived out the clear biblical teaching that God and God's faithful people are on the side of the poor.

Today I am a little less certain that Jesus was consciously announcing the Jubilee, although that is certainly possible. And today I would use an inclusive biblical translation like the New International Version.

The emergence of theologies of liberation—whether Black, feminist, or Latin American—is probably the most significant theological development of our decade. At the heart of liberation theology is the attempt fundamentally to rethink theology from the standpoint of the poor and oppressed. The central theological foundation of this approach is the thesis that God is on the side of the poor and oppressed.

It is that basic thesis that I want to probe in this short paper. The time is too limited to develop a comprehensive evangelical theology of liberation. Instead, I want to answer two questions: How biblical is the view that God is on the side of the poor and the oppressed? And, in light of the answer to this first question, how biblical is evangelical theology? I want to argue that one of the central biblical doctrines is that God is on the side of the poor and the oppressed. Tragically, evangelical theology has largely ignored this central biblical doctrine, and thus our theology has been unbiblical—indeed even heretical—at this important point.

Before I develop this double thesis, however, I want to outline some things I do not mean when I say that God is on the side of the poor and oppressed.

I do not mean that material poverty is a biblical ideal. This glorious creation is a wonderful gift from our Creator. God wants us to revel in its glory and splendor.

Second, I do not mean that the poor and oppressed are, because they are poor and oppressed, to be idealized or automatically included in the church. The poor sinfully disobey God in the same way we wretched middle-class sinners do, and they therefore need to enter into a living personal relationship with Jesus Christ. Only then do they become a part of the church. One of the serious weaknesses in much of liberation theology is an inadequate ecclesiology, especially the tendency to blur the distinction between the church and the world. And one can see why. It is understandable that Black and Latin American theologians would be impressed by the double fact that whereas most of the organized church regularly ignores the injustice that causes poverty and oppression, those who do care enough to risk their lives for improved conditions are often people who explicitly reject Christianity. Hence one can understand why someone like Hugo Assmann would conclude,

> The true Church is "the conscious emergence and the more explicit enacting of the one meaning of the one history," in other words, a revolutionary consciousness and commitment. The explicit reference to Jesus Christ becomes in this view gratuitous in the original sense of the word—something which is not demanded by or needed for the struggle of socio-economic liberation. The reference to Jesus Christ does not add "extra" to the historical struggle but is totally and without rest identified with it.[1]

In spite of deep appreciation for the factors that lead to an identification of the church with the poor and oppressed or the revolutionary minority that seeks liberation for them, one must insist that such a view is fundamentally unbiblical.

Third, when I say that God is on the side of the poor and oppressed, I do not mean that God cares more about the salvation of the poor than the salvation of the rich, or that the poor have a special claim to the gospel. It is sheer nonsense to say with Enzo Gatti, "The human areas that are poorest in every way are the most qualified for receiving the Saving Word. They are the ones that have the best right to that Word; they are the privileged recipients of the Gospel."[2] God cares equally about the salvation of the rich and the poor. To be sure, at a psychological level, Gatti is partly correct. Church growth theorists have discovered what Jesus alluded to long ago in his comment on the camel going through the eye of the needle. It is extremely difficult for rich persons to enter the kingdom. The poor are generally more ready to accept the gospel than the rich.[3] But that does not mean that God desires the salvation of the poor more than the salvation of the rich.

Fourth, to say that God is on the side of the poor is not to say that knowing God is nothing more than seeking justice for the poor and oppressed. Some—although certainly not most—liberation theologians do jump to this radical conclusion. José Miranda says bluntly, "To know Jaweh is to achieve justice for the poor."[4] He adds, "The God who does not allow himself to be objectified, because only in the immediate command of conscience is he God, clearly specifies that he is knowable *exclusively* in the cry of the poor and the weak who seek justice."[5] Tragically, it is precisely Miranda's kind of one-sided, reductionist approach that offers comfortable North Americans a plausible excuse for ignoring the radical biblical word that seeking justice for the poor is inseparable from—even though it is not identical with—knowing Yahweh.

Finally, when I say that God is on the side of the poor, I do not mean that hermeneutically we must start with some ideologically interpreted context of oppression (for instance, a Marxist definition of the poor and their oppressed situation) and then reinterpret Scripture from that ideological perspective. Black theologian James H. Cone's developing thought is interesting at this point. In 1969 in *Black Theology and Black Power*, he wrote, "The fact that I am Black is my ultimate reality. My identity with *blackness*, and what it means for millions living in a white world, controls the investigation. It is impossible for me to surrender this basic reality for a 'higher, more universal reality.'"[6]

By the time Cone wrote *God of the Oppressed*, however, he realized that such a view would relativize all theological claims, including his own critique of white racist theology. "How do we distinguish our words about God from God's Word? Unless this question is answered satisfactorily, Black theologians' distinction between white theology and Black Theology is vulnerable to the white contention that the latter is merely the ideological justification of radical Black politics."[7] To be sure, Cone believes as strongly as other liberation theologians that the hermeneutical key to Scripture is God's saving action to liberate the oppressed. But how does he know that?

> In God's revelation in Scripture we come to the recognition that the divine liberation of the oppressed is not determined by our perceptions but by the God of the Exodus, the prophets, and Jesus Christ who calls the oppressed into a liberated existence. Divine revelation *alone* is the test of the validity of this starting point. And if it can be shown that God as witnessed in the Scriptures is not the liberator of the oppressed, then Black Theology would have either to drop the "Christian" designation or to choose another starting point.[8]

One can only wish all liberation theologians agreed with Cone!

When then I say that God is on the side of the poor, I do not mean that poverty is the ideal; that the poor and oppressed qua poor and oppressed are the church or have a special right to hear the gospel; that seeking justice for the oppressed is identical with knowing Yahweh; or that hermeneutically one should begin with some ideologically interpreted context of oppression and then reinterpret Scripture from that perspective.

In what sense, then, is God on the side of the poor and oppressed? I want to develop three points:[9]

1. At the central points of revelation history, God acted to liberate the poor and oppressed.

2. God acts in history to exalt the poor and oppressed and to cast down the rich and oppressive.

3. God's people, if they are truly God's people, are also on the side of the poor and oppressed.

First, I want to look briefly at three central points of revelation history—the exodus, the destruction of Israel and Judah, and the incarnation. At the central moments when God displayed his mighty acts in history to reveal his nature and will, God also intervened to liberate the poor and oppressed. God displayed his power at the exodus to free oppressed slaves. When God called Moses at the burning bush, he informed Moses that his intention was to end suffering and injustice: "I have seen the affliction of my people who are in Egypt, and have heard their cry because of their taskmasters; I know their sufferings, and I have come down to deliver them out of the hand of the Egyptians" (Exodus 3:7-8, RSV). Each year at the harvest festival, the Israelites repeated a liturgical confession celebrating the way God had acted to free a poor, oppressed people.

> A wandering Aramean was my father; and he went down into Egypt and sojourned there. . . . And the Egyptians treated us harshly, and afflicted us, and laid upon us hard bondage. Then we cried to the LORD, the God of our fathers, and the LORD heard our voice, and saw our affliction, our toil, and our oppression; and the LORD brought us out of Egypt with a mighty hand. (Deuteronomy 26:5-8, RSV)

Unfortunately, some liberation theologians see in the exodus only God's liberation of an oppressed people and miss the fact that God also acted to fulfill his promises to Abraham, to reveal his will, and to call out a special people. Certainly, God acted at the exodus to call a special people so that through them God could reveal his will and bring salvation to all people. But God's will included the fact, as he revealed ever more clearly to his covenant people, that his people should follow him and side with the poor and oppressed.

The fact that Yahweh did not liberate all poor Egyptians at the exodus does not mean that God was not concerned for the poor

7

everywhere any more than the fact that God did not give the Ten Commandments to everyone in the Near East means that God did not intend them to have universal significance. Because God chose to reveal himself in history, God disclosed to particular people at particular points in time what God willed for all people everywhere. At the exodus, God acted to demonstrate that God is opposed to oppression. We distort the biblical interpretation of the momentous event of the exodus unless we see that at this pivotal point, the Lord of the universe was at work correcting oppression and liberating the poor.

The prophets' explanation for the destruction of Israel and then Judah underlines the same point. The explosive message of the prophets is that God destroyed Israel not just because of idolatry (although certainly because of that) but also because of economic exploitation and mistreatment of the poor!

The middle of the eighth century BC was a time of political success and economic prosperity unknown since the days of Solomon. But it was precisely at this moment that God sent the prophet Amos to announce the unwelcome news that the northern kingdom would be destroyed. Why? Penetrating beneath the facade of current prosperity and fantastic economic growth, Amos saw terrible oppression of the poor. He saw the rich "trample the head of the poor into the dust of the earth" (Amos 2:7, RSV). He saw that the affluent lifestyle of the rich was built on oppression of the poor (6:1-7). Even in the courts the poor had no hope, because the rich bribed the judges (5:10-15).

God's word through Amos was that the northern kingdom would be destroyed and the people taken into exile (7:11, 17). Only a very few years after Amos spoke, it happened just as God had said. Because of their mistreatment of the poor, God destroyed the northern kingdom. If there were time, it would be easy to document the same point with reference to the destruction of the southern kingdom (e.g., Jeremiah 5:26-29; 34:3-17). The cataclysmic catastrophe of national destruction and captivity reveals that the God of the exodus was still at work correcting the oppression of the poor.

When God acted to reveal himself most completely in the incarnation, God continued to demonstrate his special concern for the poor and oppressed. Luke used the programmatic account of Jesus in the synagogue at Nazareth to define Jesus' mission. The words Jesus read from the prophet Isaiah are familiar to us all: "The Spirit of the Lord is upon me, because he has anointed me to preach good news to the poor. He has sent me to proclaim release to the captives and recovery of sight to the blind, to set at liberty those who are oppressed, to proclaim the acceptable year of the Lord" (Luke 4:18-19, RSV). After reading these words, Jesus informed his audience that this Scripture was now fulfilled in himself. The mission of the Incarnate One was to preach the Good News to the poor and free the oppressed.

Many people spiritualize these words either by simplistically assuming that Jesus was talking about healing blinded hearts in captivity to sin or by appealing to the later Old Testament and intertestamental idea of "the poor of Yahweh" (the *'anawim*). It is true that the later psalms and the intertestamental literature use the terms for the poor (especially *'anawim*) to refer to pious, humble, devout Israelites who place all their trust in Yahweh.[10] But that does not mean that this usage had no connection with socioeconomic poverty. Indeed, it was precisely the fact that the economically poor and oppressed were the faithful remnant who trusted in Yahweh that led to the new usage where the words for the poor designated the pious faithful.

The Hebrew words for the poor were *'ani, 'anaw, 'ebyon, dal,* and *ras. 'Ani* (and *'anaw,* which originally had approximately the same basic meaning) denotes one who is "wrongfully impoverished or dispossessed."[11] *'Ebyon* refers to a beggar imploring charity. *Dal* connotes a thin, weakly person, for example, an

9

impoverished, deprived peasant.[12] Unlike the others, *ras* is an essentially neutral term. In their persistent polemic against the oppression of the poor, the prophets used the terms *'ebyon*, *'ani*, and *dal*.

Later these same words (especially *'anawim*) were used to designate the faithful remnant, the "pious poor" who trust solely in Yahweh.[13] But that does not mean that the older socioeconomic connotations were lost. Richard Batey puts it this way:

> Beginning with the experience that the poor were often oppressed by the wicked rich, the poor were considered to be the special objects of Yahweh's protection and deliverance (Psalm 9:18; 19:1-8. . .). Therefore the poor looked to Yahweh as the source of deliverance from their enemies and oppressors. This attitude of trust and dependence exemplified that piety that should have characterized every Israelite. In this way the concept of the "pious poor" developed.[14]

The New International Dictionary of New Testament Theology makes the same point:

> Only in the setting of this historical situation can we understand the meaning in the Psalms of "poor" and "needy." The poor man is the one who suffers injustice; he is poor because others have despised God's law. He therefore turns, helpless and humble, to God in prayer. . . . Through the self-identification, generation after generation, of those who prayed with the poor in psalms of individual lamentation and thanksgiving . . . there gradually developed the specific connotation of "poor" as meaning all those who turn to God in great need and seek his help. God is praised as the protector of the poor (e.g., Psalm 72:2, 4, 121; 132:15), who procures justice for them against their oppressors.[15]

This same usage is common in intertestamental literature. When Greece and then Rome conquered Palestine, Hellenistic culture and values were foisted upon the Jews. Those who remained faithful to Yahweh often suffered financially.

Thus the term *poor* was, as J. A. Ziesler says, "virtually equivalent to pious, God-fearing, and godly and reflects a situation where the rich were mainly those who had sold out to the incoming culture and had allowed their religious devotion to become corrupted by the new ways. If the poor were the pious, the faithful and largely oppressed, the rich were the powerful, ungodly, worldly, even apostate."[16] Thus the faithful remnant at Qumran called themselves "the poor" (*ebyon*).[17] And they and other first-century Jews yearned eagerly for the new age when the Messiah would come to fulfill the messianic promises (e.g., Isaiah 11:4) and bring justice to the poor.[18]

Thus, when Jesus read from Isaiah 61 in the synagogue at Nazareth and proclaimed Good News to the poor, he was announcing to the faithful remnant who trusted in Yahweh and therefore were also poor socioeconomically, that the messianic age of justice for the poor had arrived.

This is confirmed by the growing evidence, developed most convincingly in a recent dissertation at the University of Basel by Robert Sloan,[19] that in citing Isaiah 61:1, Jesus intended to proclaim the eschatological Jubilee. Sloan cites a Qumran document that comes from roughly the same time as Jesus. This text links the Jubilee passage of Leviticus 25 and the Sabbatical release of debts of Deuteronomy 15 with Isaiah 61:1. Furthermore, it gives the Isaiah passage a specific Jubilee interpretation. Equally important, all three texts are placed in an eschatological perspective. Thus, the Qumran text expects the economic and social reordering described in Leviticus 25, Deuteronomy 15, and Isaiah 61 to occur when the Messiah ushers in the new age. In fact, Sloan has discovered that in Jewish literature, the Jubilee text is almost always placed in an eschatological context. A similar interpretation would seem to be appropriate for Luke 4:16-21. This means that at the heart of Jesus' message was the announcement that the messianic age of eschatological expectation was beginning in his life and ministry ("Today this Scripture has been fulfilled in your hearing"; v. 21, RSV). At the very core of Jesus' conception of the new messianic age, then, was the economic reordering, the special concern for the poor, the release of captives and liberation of the oppressed called for in the Jubilee. The messianic age that he saw himself inaugurating had specific economic and social content.

Other aspects of Jesus' teaching support this interpretation. The Lucan Beatitudes promise blessing to the poor and hungry. The messianic kingdom in which the pious, but therefore also socio-economically poor, will receive justice is now coming in the person of Jesus. Nor does Matthew represent a spiritualized version of the Beatitudes.[20] The poor "in spirit" are the pious poor who are also socioeconomically deprived. And they hunger and thirst for righteousness—that is, justice! As Herman Ridderbos rightly insists, the word "righteousness" here "must not be understood in the Pauline forensic sense of imputed forensic righteousness, but as the kingly justice which will be brought to light one day for the salvation of the oppressed and the outcasts, and which will be executed especially by the Messiah. . . . It is *this* justice to which the 'poor in spirit' and 'the meek' look forward in the Sermon on the Mount."[21]

Now, I do not in any way want to imply that Jesus' message was limited to proclaiming the eschatological Jubilee or that his mission focused exclusively on socioeconomic concerns. His message included a central concern for forgiving sinners, and he came to die on the cross for our sins. But it simply will not do to spiritualize Jesus' message and overlook the fact that right at the heart of the mission of the Incarnate One was a concern for justice for the poor and oppressed. His strong warning that those who do not feed the hungry, clothe the naked, and visit the prisoners will experience eternal damnation (Matthew 25:31-46) does not represent a peripheral concern. It represents a central focus of his messianic mission.

At the supreme moment of history, when God himself took on human flesh, we see the God of Israel still at work liberating the poor and oppressed and summoning his people to do the same.

The second aspect of the biblical teaching that God is on the side of the poor and oppressed is that God works in history to cast down the rich and exalt the poor.

Mary's Magnificat puts it simply and bluntly:

> My soul magnifies the Lord. . . .
> He has put down the mighty from their thrones,
>   and exalted those of low degree;
> he has filled the hungry with good things,
>   and the rich he has sent empty away.
> —Luke 1:46-53, RSV

The statement in James 5:1 (RSV), "Come now, you rich, weep and howl for the miseries that are coming upon you," is a constant theme of biblical revelation.

Why does Scripture declare that God regularly reverses the good fortunes of the rich? Is God engaged in class warfare? Actually, our texts never say that God loves the poor more than the rich. But they do constantly assert that God lifts up the poor and disadvantaged. And they persistently insist that God casts down the wealthy and powerful. Why? Precisely because, according to Scripture, the rich often become wealthy by oppressing the poor and because they fail to feed the hungry.

Why did James warn the rich to weep and howl because of impending misery? Because they had cheated their workers: "You have laid up treasure for the last days. Behold, the wages of the laborers who mowed your fields, which you kept back by fraud, cry out; and the cries of the harvesters have reached the ears of the Lord of hosts. You have lived on the earth in luxury and in pleasure; you have fattened your hearts in a day of slaughter" (James 5:3-5, RSV). God does not have class enemies. But God hates and punishes injustice and neglect of the poor. If we accept the repeated warnings of Scripture, the rich are frequently guilty of both.

Long before the days of James, Jeremiah knew that the rich were often rich because of oppression.

> Wicked men are found among my people;
> they lurk like fowlers lying in wait.
> They set a trap;
> they catch men.
> Like a basket full of birds,
> their houses are full of treachery;
> *therefore, they have become great and rich,*
> *they have grown fat and sleek.*
> They know no bounds in deeds of wickedness;
> they judge not with justice
> the cause of the fatherless, to make it prosper,
> and they do not defend the rights of the needy.
> Shall I not punish them for these things?
>   says the LORD.
>   —Jeremiah 5:26-29, RSV (emphasis added)

Hosea and Micah made similar charges:

> A trader, in whose hand are false balances,
> he loves to oppress.
> Ephraim has said, "Ah, but I am rich,
> I have gained wealth for myself";

but all his riches can never offset
 the guilt he has incurred.
—Hosea 12:7-8, RSV

The voice of the LORD cries to the city. . . .
Can I forget the treasures of wickedness in the house of the
wicked,
and the scant measure that is accursed?
Shall I acquit the men with wicked scales
 and with a bag of deceitful weights?
Your rich men are full of violence.
—Micah 6:9-12, RSV

Job 24:1-12; Psalm 73:2-12; Ezekiel 22:23-29; and Amos
8:4-8—to cite just a few more texts—all repeat the same point.

One more example from Isaiah is important. Through the
prophet, God declared that the rulers of Judah were rich because
they had cheated the poor. Surfeited with affluence, the wealthy
women had indulged in self-centered wantonness, oblivious to the
suffering of the oppressed. The result, God said, would be devastating destruction.

The LORD enters into judgment
 with the elders and princes of his people:
"It is you who have devoured the vineyard,
 the spoil of the poor is in your houses.
What do you mean by crushing my people,
 by grinding the face of the poor?" says the LORD of hosts.
—Isaiah 3:14-15, RSV (emphasis added)

Because the rich oppress the poor and weak, the Lord of history is at work pulling down their houses and kingdoms. Sometimes
Scripture does not charge the rich with direct oppression of the

poor. It simply accuses them of failure to share with the needy. But the result is the same.

The biblical explanation of Sodom's destruction provides one illustration of this terrible truth. If asked why Sodom was destroyed, virtually all Christians would point to the city's gross sexual perversity. But that is a one-sided recollection of what Scripture actually teaches. Ezekiel shows that one important reason God destroyed Sodom was because she stubbornly refused to share with the poor! "Behold, this was the guilt of your sister Sodom: she and her daughters had pride, *surfeit of food, and prosperous ease, but did not aid the poor and needy.* They were haughty, and did abominable things before me; therefore, I removed them when I saw it" (Ezekiel 16:49-50, RSV; emphasis added). The text does not say that they oppressed the poor (although they probably did). It simply accuses them of failing to assist the needy.

The third aspect of the biblical teaching that God is on the side of the poor and oppressed is that the people of God, if they are really the people of God, are also on the side of the poor and oppressed. Those who neglect the poor and the oppressed are not really God's people at all—no matter how frequent their religious rituals or how orthodox their creeds and confessions. The prophets sometimes made this point by insisting that knowledge of God and seeking justice for the oppressed are inseparable. At other times they condemned the religious rituals of the oppressors who tried to worship God and still continued to oppress the poor.

Jeremiah announced God's harsh message that King Jehoiakim did not know Yahweh and would be destroyed because of his injustice:

> Woe to him who builds his house by unrighteousness,
> and his upper rooms by injustice;
> who makes his neighbor serve him for nothing,
> and does not give him his wages. . . .

Did not your father eat and drink
and do justice and righteousness?
Then it was well with him.
He judged the cause of the poor and needy;
    then it was well.
Is not this to know me?
says the LORD.
—Jeremiah 22:13-16, RSV

Knowing God necessarily involves seeking justice for the poor and needy (cf. also Hosea 2:19-20).

The same correlation between seeking justice for the poor and knowledge of God is equally clear in the messianic passage of Isaiah 11:1-9. Of the shoot of the stump of Jesse, the prophet says, "With righteousness he shall judge the poor, and decide with equity for the meek of the earth" (v. 4). In this ultimate messianic shalom, "the earth shall be full of the knowledge of the LORD as the waters cover the sea" (v. 9, RSV).

The prophets also announced God's outrage against worship in the context of mistreatment of the poor and disadvantaged. Isaiah denounced Israel (he called her Sodom and Gomorrah!) because she tried to worship Yahweh and oppress the weak at the same time.

"Why have we fasted, and thou seest it not?
Why have we humbled ourselves, and thou takest no knowledge of it?"
Behold, in the day of your fast *you seek your own pleasure*,
and oppress all your workers. . . .
Is not this the fast that I choose:
    to loose the bonds of wickedness,
    to undo the thongs of the yoke,
to let the oppressed go free,
    and to break every yoke?

Is it not to share your bread with the hungry,
    and bring the homeless poor into your house?
—Isaiah 58:3-7; cf. Isaiah 1:10-17, RSV

God's words through the prophet Amos are also harsh:

I hate, I despise your feasts,
and I take no delight in your solemn assemblies.
Even though you offer me your burnt offerings and cereal
offerings,
I will not accept them. . . .
But let justice roll down like waters,
and righteousness like an everflowing stream.
—Amos 5:21-24, RSV

Earlier in the chapter, Amos had condemned the rich and powerful for oppressing the poor. They even bribed judges to prevent redress in the courts. God wants justice, not mere religious rituals, from such people. Their worship is a mockery and abomination to the God of the poor.

Nor has God changed. Jesus repeated the same theme. He warned the people about scribes who secretly oppress widows while making a public display of their piety. Their pious-looking garments and frequent visits to the synagogue are a sham. Woe to religious hypocrites "who devour widows' houses and for a pretense make long prayers" (Mark 12:38-40, RSV). Like Amos and Isaiah, Jesus announced that God is outraged by those who try to mix pious practices and mistreatment of the poor.

The prophetic word against religious hypocrites raises an extremely difficult question. Are the people of God truly God's people if they oppress the poor? Is the church really the church if it does not work to free the oppressed?

We have seen how God declared through the prophet Isaiah that the people of Israel were really Sodom and Gomorrah rather than the people of God (1:10). God simply could not tolerate their idolatry and their exploitation of the poor and disadvantaged any longer. Jesus was even sharper and blunter. To those who do not feed the hungry, clothe the naked, and visit the prisoners, he will speak a terrifying word at the final judgment: "Depart from me, you cursed, into the eternal fire prepared for the devil and his angels" (Matthew 25:41, RSV). The meaning is clear: Jesus intends for his disciples to imitate his own special concern for the poor and needy. Those who disobey will experience eternal damnation.

But perhaps we have misinterpreted Matthew 25. Some people think that "the least of these" (v. 45, RSV) and "the least of these my brethren" (v. 40, RSV) refer only to Christians. This exegesis is not certain. But even if the primary reference of these words is to poor believers, other aspects of Jesus' teaching not only permit but require us to extend the meaning of Matthew 25 to both believers and unbelievers who are poor and oppressed. The story of the good Samaritan (Luke 10:29-37) teaches that anybody in need is our neighbor. Matthew 5:43-48 is even more explicit: "You have heard that it was said, 'You shall love your neighbor and hate your enemy.' But I say to you, love your enemies and pray for those who persecute you, so that you may be sons of your Father who is in heaven; for he makes his sun rise on the evil and on the good, and sends rain on the just and on the unjust."

The ideal in the Qumran community (known to us through the Dead Sea Scrolls) was indeed to "love all the sons of light" and "hate all the sons of darkness" (1 QS 1:9-10). Even in the Old Testament, Israelites were commanded to love the neighbor who was the son of their own people and ordered not to seek the prosperity of Ammonites and Moabites (Leviticus 19:17-18; Deuteronomy 23:3-6). But Jesus explicitly forbids his followers to limit their loving concern to the neighbor who is a member of

19

their own ethnic or religious group. He commands his followers to imitate God, who does good for all people everywhere. As George Ladd has said, "Jesus redefines the meaning of love for neighbor; it means love for any man in need."[22] In light of the parable of the good Samaritan and the clear teaching of Matthew 5:43-48, one is compelled to say that part of the full teaching of Matthew 25 is that those who fail to aid the poor and oppressed (whether or not they are believers) are simply not the people of God.

Lest we forget the warning, God repeats it in 1 John: "If any one has the world's goods and sees his brother in need, yet closes his heart against him, how does God's love abide in him? Little children, let us not love in word or speech but in deed and in truth" (3:17-18; cf. also, James 2:14-17). Again, the words are plain. What do they mean for Western Christians who demand increasing affluence each year while people in the third world suffer malnutrition, deformed bodies and brains, even starvation? The text clearly says that if we fail to aid the needy, we do not have God's love—no matter what we may say. The texts demand deeds, not pious phrases and saintly speeches. Regardless of what we do or say at 11:00 on Sunday morning, if we neglect the poor and oppressed, we are not the people of God.

But still the question persists. Are professing believers no longer Christians because of continuing sin? Obviously not. The Christian knows that sinful selfishness continues to plague even the most saintly. We are the people of God not because of our own righteousness but solely because of Christ's death for us.

That response is extremely important and very true. But it is also inadequate. All the texts from both testaments that we have just surveyed surely mean more than that the people of God are disobedient (but still justified all the same) when they neglect the poor. These verses pointedly assert that some people so disobey God that they are not his people at all in spite of their pious profession. Neglect of the poor is one of the oft-repeated biblical signs of such disobedience. Certainly, none of us would claim that we fulfill Matthew 25 perfectly. And we cling to the hope of forgiveness. But there comes a point—and thank God, he alone knows where—when neglect of the poor is no longer forgiven. It is punished. Eternally.

In light of this clear biblical teaching, how biblical is our evangelical theology? Certainly there have been some great moments of faithfulness. John Wesley's, William Wilberforce's, and Charles Finney's evangelical abolitionists stood solidly in the biblical tradition in their search for justice for the poor and oppressed of their time. But twentieth-century evangelicals have not, by and large, followed their example. I think we must confess that the evangelical community is largely on the side of the rich oppressors rather than the oppressed poor.

Imagine what would happen if all our evangelical institutions— our youth organizations, our publications, our colleges and seminaries, our congregations and denominational headquarters— would all dare to undertake a comprehensive two-year examination of their programs and activities to answer this question: "Is there the same balance and emphasis on justice for the poor and oppressed in our programs as there is in Scripture?" I am willing to predict that if we did that with an unconditional readiness to change whatever did not correspond with the scriptural revelation of God's special concern for the poor and oppressed, we would unleash a new movement of biblical social concern that would change the course of modern history.

But our problem is not primarily one of ethics. It is not that we have failed to live what our teachers have taught. Our theology itself has been unbiblical and therefore heretical. I think James Cone is right when he says,

> When church theologians, from the time of Constantine to the present, failed to see the ethical impact of the biblical God

for the liberation of the oppressed, that failure occurred because of defective theology. To understand correctly the church's ethical mistake, we must see it in connection with a prior theological mistake.

Theologians of the Christian church have not interpreted Christian ethics as an act for the liberation of the oppressed because their views of divine revelation were defined by philosophy and other cultural values rather than by the biblical theme of God as the liberator of the oppressed. . . . We cannot say that Luther, Calvin, Wesley, and other prominent representatives of the church's traditions were limited by their time, as if their ethical judgments on oppression did not affect the essential truth of their theologies. They were wrong ethically because they were wrong theologically. They were wrong theologically because they failed to listen to the Bible.[23]

By largely ignoring the central biblical teaching that God is on the side of the poor, evangelical theology has been profoundly unorthodox. The Bible has just as much to say about this doctrine as it does about Jesus' resurrection. And yet we evangelicals insist on the resurrection as a criterion of orthodoxy and largely ignore the equally prominent biblical teaching that God is on the side of the poor and the oppressed.

Now please do not misunderstand me at this point. I am not saying that the resurrection is unimportant. The bodily resurrection of Jesus of Nazareth is absolutely central to Christian faith, and anyone who denies it or says it is unimportant has fallen into heresy. But if centrality in Scripture is any criterion of doctrinal importance, then the biblical teaching that God is on the side of the poor ought to be an extremely important doctrine for evangelicals.

I am afraid evangelicals have fallen into theological liberalism. Of course, we usually think of theological liberalism in terms of classical nineteenth-century liberals who denied the deity, the atonement, and the bodily resurrection of Jesus our Lord. And that is correct. People who abandon those central biblical doctrines have fallen into terrible heresy.

But notice what the essence of theological liberalism is—it is allowing our thinking and living to be shaped by surrounding society's views and values rather than by biblical revelation. Liberal theologians thought that belief in the deity of Jesus Christ and his bodily resurrection was incompatible with a modern scientific worldview. So they followed surrounding "scientific" society rather than Scripture.

Evangelicals rightly called attention to this heresy—and then tragically made exactly the same move in another area. We have allowed the values of our affluent, materialistic society to shape our thinking and acting toward the poor.

It is much easier in evangelical circles today to insist on an orthodox Christology than to insist on the biblical teaching that God is on the side of the poor. We have allowed our theology to be shaped by the economic preferences of our materialistic contemporaries rather than by Scripture. And that is to fall into theological liberalism. We have not been nearly as orthodox as we have claimed.

Past failure, however, is no reason for despair. I think we mean it when we sing, "I'd rather have Jesus than houses or lands." I think we mean it when we write and affirm doctrinal statements that boldly declare that we will not only believe but also live whatever Scripture teaches. But if we do mean it, then we must teach and live, in a world full of injustice and starvation, the important biblical doctrine that God and his faithful people are on the side of the poor and oppressed. Unless we drastically reshape both our theology and our entire institutional church life so that the fact that God is on the side of the poor and oppressed becomes as central to evangelical theology and evangelical institutional programs as it is in Scripture, we will demonstrate to the world that our verbal commitment to *sola scriptura* is a dishonest ideological support for an unjust, materialistic status quo. But I hope and believe that in the next decade, millions of evangelicals will allow the biblical teaching that God is on the side of the poor and oppressed to fundamentally reshape our culturally conditioned theology and our unbiblically one-sided programs and institutions. If that happens, we will forge a new truly evangelical theology of liberation that will change the course of modern history.

Notes

1. José Miguez Bonino, *Doing Theology in a Revolutionary Situation* (Philadelphia: Fortress, 1975), 161–62.

2. Enzo Gatti, *Rich Church—Poor Church? Some Biblical Perspectives* (Maryknoll, NY: Orbis, 1974), 43.

3. See Samuel Escobar's summary of Donald McGavran in Samuel Escobar and John Driver, *Christian Mission and Social Justice* (Scottsdale, PA: Herald, 1978), 45–47.

4. José Miranda, *Marx and the Bible: A Critique of the Philosophy of Oppression* (Maryknoll, NY: Orbis, 1974), 44.

5. Miranda, 48.

6. James H. Cone, *Black Theology and Black Power* (New York: Seabury, 1969), 32–33. But see a conflicting, more biblical emphasis on pp. 34, 51.

7. James H. Cone, *God of the Oppressed* (New York: Seabury, 1975), 84.

8. Cone, 82; italics in original.

9. The following section relies heavily on chapter 3 of my *Rich Christians in an Age of Hunger: A Biblical Study* (Downers Grove, IL: InterVarsity, 1977).

10. See Richard Batey, *Jesus and the Poor: The Poverty Program of the First Christians* (New York: Harper, 1972), 83–97; Albert Gelin, *The Poor of Yahweh* (Collegeville, MN: Liturgical, 1964). See also Carl Schultz, "'*Ani* and *Anaw* in Psalms" (unpublished PhD diss., Brandeis University, 1973); Peter D. Miscall, "The Concept of the Poor in the Old Testament" (unpublished PhD diss., Harvard University, 1972).

11. Gerhard Kittel and Gerhard Friedrich, eds., *Theological Dictionary of the New Testament*, 10 vols. (Grand Rapids: Eerdmans, 1964–76), 6:888. Hereafter *TDNT*.

12. Gelin, *Poor of Yahweh*, 19–20.

13. Gelin, 50.

14. Batey, *Jesus and the Poor*, 92.

15. Colin Brown, ed., *The New International Dictionary of New Testament Theology*, 3 vols. (Grand Rapids: Zondervan, 1976), 2:822–23.

16. J. A. Ziesler, *Christian Asceticism* (Grand Rapids: Eerdmans, 1973), 52.

17. *TDNT*, 6:896–99.

18. Batey, *Jesus and the Poor*, 93; *TDNT*, 6:895.

19. Robert Sloan, *The Favorable Year of the Lord: A Study of Jubilary Theology in the Gospel of Luke* (Austin, TX: Schola, 1977).

20. See *TDNT*, 6:904n175.

21. Herman Ridderbos, *The Coming of the Kingdom* (Philadelphia: Presbyterians Reformed, 1962), 190.

22. George E. Ladd, *A Theology of the New Testament* (Grand Rapids: Eerdmans, 1974), 133.

23. Cone, *God of the Oppressed*, 199–200.

CHAPTER 2

An Evangelical Witness
for Peace

I prepared this short speech to present at the Rose Bowl
in Pasadena, California, on June 6, 1982. According to
the *Los Angeles Times*, about eighty-five thousand people packed the Rose Bowl to call for nuclear disarmament that day. Prominent singers who performed included Bob Dylan, Stevie Wonder, Joan Baez, and Linda
Ronstadt. The speakers included Jesse Jackson, Cesar
Chavez, Jane Fonda, Patti Davis (President Ronald
Reagan's daughter), Rev. James Lawson (Martin Luther
King Jr.'s colleague), Bishop James Armstrong (president
of the National Council of Churches), and Muhammad
Ali. The detailed program indicates that I (and most of
the other speakers) had only three minutes, so I probably actually delivered only a portion of this speech.

The danger of nuclear war seemed to decrease after the
collapse of the Soviet Union and the end of the Cold War.
But it's clear even today that nuclear war remains a threat.

I am honored to be here as president of Evangelicals for Social
Action, a national movement of evangelical Christians committed
to stopping the nuclear arms race.

I am also honored to be here as an evangelical Christian. Now,
we all know that some very visible, very vocal evangelical leaders
support President Reagan's massive military buildup. But among

26

evangelical Christians, they do not represent a majority. Most evangelical Christians want the arms race stopped. Most evangelical Christians are proud of Billy Graham's courageous peace pilgrimage to Moscow in spite of vigorous opposition from the US State Department. More and more evangelical Christians are coming to the conclusion that nuclear war could never be justified. In fact, President Reagan's pastor, the Reverend Donn Moomaw of Bel Air Presbyterian Church, a well-known evangelical, said in a recent sermon, "Because nuclear weapons are so destructive, so devastating, so final . . . they are morally indefensible. I must be a nuclear pacifist."

I am honored to be here finally as a citizen of our diverse, pluralistic society. We come together today as Baptists and Buddhists, Catholics and charismatics, Jews and Jesuits, humanists and Hindus, Muslims and Methodists to say no to nuclear madness. Each of us has our own way of explaining why our deepest beliefs compel us to oppose the arms race. Because we all respect one another's different traditions, we need to share with each other the diverse bases of our common concern for peace. Briefly then, permit me to share why I as an evangelical Christian believe that continuing with the nuclear arms race would be one of the most immoral decisions in history.

Christians believe that the good earth, all life, and you and I are the creation of a personal, loving God. I do not believe that persons and nature have resulted from the accidental combination of subatomic matter in a blind materialistic process. If that were true, persons would merely be complex machines, and ethical values even about peacemaking would be totally subjective products of blind chance. Certainly, the Creator used a gloriously complex evolutionary process stretching over vast geological ages to create the world. But it was not an accident.

The almighty Creator is an infinite person who wants to be in free, loving relationship with finite persons. So the Creator molded you and me in the divine image. That is why I believe every person is of infinite value. The worth of individuals does not depend on their productivity or usefulness to society. Every person is created in God's image for personal relationship with the Lord of the universe. That is why it is wrong for communist totalitarians to sacrifice millions of people for the alleged benefit of the state. That is why it is wrong for American and Russian militarists to build megaton weapons that will destroy people by the hundreds of millions.

Not just persons, but the earth itself also comes from the Creator's loving hand. As I worked on my book *Nuclear Holocaust and Christian Hope*, my love for the gorgeous beauty of the earth grew deeper and deeper. As I faced the stark reality that human madness might very well destroy our little planet in my lifetime, I fell more deeply in love with the soft gentle breezes, the towering redwoods, the majestic Rockies, and the purple sunsets. Christians believe the earth is a ring from the Beloved to be cherished and preserved, not an accidental commodity to be exploited and destroyed. To continue down the path that makes nuclear destruction ever more likely reflects not merely callous contempt for future generations; it also demonstrates a blasphemous affront to the Creator of this gorgeous, fragile planet.

The Creator intended persons to live together in harmonious human society, shaping cultures and civilizations of beauty, justice, and peace. But human history is a tragic mixture of good and evil. So often human greed, national pride, and sheer selfishness have led to ghastly conflict. Choosing to deny that we are made for obedient relationship with God, choosing to love ourselves more than our neighbors, we have created an upward spiral of violence. Clubs gave way to cannons, firebombs to twenty-megaton nuclear warheads. Today we stand trembling at the precipice, peering fearfully into the nuclear abyss.

But still, my friends, I have hope. I believe that it is possible to attain nuclear disarmament in the next twenty-five years. But the

basis of my hope is not primarily the growing anti-nuclear movement, although I am deeply involved in and highly grateful for
that movement. The basis of my hope is God.

Christian faith reminds me that God has taken the initiative to
correct all that is evil and unjust in the world. Christians believe
that the Creator of the galaxies actually took on human flesh and
walked the dusty paths of Palestine as a humble teacher. He
taught that we should be peacemakers and love our enemies. He
cared for the poor and the weak, the sick and the social outcasts,
whom the powerful always ignore. And he said that God loves
even the people who have messed up their lives the worst, even
those who have fallen into the grossest selfishness and sin. And
then he took one incredible additional step. He said he was going
to die for precisely those kinds of people.

His radical acceptance of those who had harmed themselves,
their families, and their neighbors was not based on some kind of
cheap indulgence. In fact, he said that harming other people is not
just an awful offense against the neighbor; it is also a terrible
affront against the Creator who created neighbors in the divine
image. Therefore, oppressors and sinners are God's enemies
because they disrupt the harmony of God's good creation. But
Jesus said God loves God's sinful enemies so much that he would
die for them. As God in the flesh, Jesus Christ said he would take
all the evil of his sinful enemies upon himself. Because he loved
them, he would take on himself the punishment they deserved for
their violence, oppression, and sins. At the cross God suffered the
agony of Roman crucifixion for sinful enemies. That is the foundation of Jesus' call to love our enemies. It is because Jesus, the
Creator of the galaxies, loves God's enemies enough to suffer
unbelievable agony for them that he taught that his followers
should also love their enemies.

But isn't that just utopian drivel? Don't we live in a violent,
vicious world where loving enemies does not work? Didn't Jesus'

life end in failure at the cross? Now, that would be the proper conclusion, except for one thing. Jesus, you see, did not stay dead. On the third day, he was alive again. On Easter morning the tomb was empty. By raising Jesus from the dead, God proved that Jesus' way of loving enemies was not naive utopianism, but God's way to peace. By raising Jesus from the dead, God proved that Jesus was correct in teaching that God was busy restoring the broken beauty of human society.

It is because I know that the Peacemaker from Nazareth rose from the dead that I have hope today. It is because I know that the Teacher of peace was God in the flesh that I dare to commit my life to the long, costly struggle for nuclear disarmament.

But I don't say that easily. I don't for a minute suppose that I can persist in the long, twenty-five-year struggle against nuclear holocaust in my own strength. Let's not kid ourselves. Nuclear disarmament will not happen in a year or two or three, even if—please, God—we can elect a president in '84 committed to nuclear disarmament rather than nationalistic superiority. If nuclear disarmament comes at all, if we succeed in avoiding nuclear holocaust, it will happen only after long, exhausting decades of costly struggle.

Why do I hope to be able to walk that long weary road? Christians believe that the risen Lord Jesus now lives in those who open their lives to him. The apostle Paul said, "I no longer live, but Christ lives in me" (Galatians 2:20, NIV). From personal experience, I know that the risen Jesus lives in me. I know that he calls me to oppose nuclear madness because creation is a divine gift to be treasured, because every human life is sacred, because God loves God's enemies and calls on me to love my enemies. I cannot do that in my own strength. But I don't have to, because Christ lives in me.

My friends, the task before us is awesome. The next two decades are the most dangerous in human history. But we can succeed. We can, I believe, rid the world of the monstrous evil of nuclear weapons. The Creator of the galaxies is on the side of peace. In realistic political terms, nuclear disarmament looks extremely difficult. But it is not impossible, for with God all things are possible. Let's join God to make the planet a little safer for your children and mine.

Reflect on ways you can make the world safer today and in the future. Involve your family, friends, and church members as you plan. You may discover new ideas and avenues to work together.

CHAPTER 3

An Evangelical Vision for American Public Life

I delivered this address on May 16, 1983, at the John F. Kennedy School of Government at Harvard University. The event was sponsored by the Institute of Politics at the Harvard Divinity School. It was the second half of a two-part program in religion and politics. Jerry Falwell had delivered the first part on April 25, 1983. I gave the lecture another thirty times in the next five years in North America, England, Germany, and Sweden.

In 1983 I was too optimistic about the size of the progressive evangelical movement I represented, I underestimated the size of the evangelical world that agreed with Jerry Falwell, and I also failed to see the widespread embrace of the religious right in the next three decades. I remain pro-life, consider abortion tragic, and want the number of abortions greatly reduced. But I would be somewhat less specific today about how best to do that. Today, as I continue to defend the civil rights of LGBTQ persons, I am much more critical and specific in my criticism of the way that most evangelicals have failed miserably to love and protect the LGBTQ community.

My vision for American public life cuts across most of the political and ideological stereotypes. I believe that, on the basis of the just war tradition, not only the use but also the very possession of nuclear weapons is immoral and unacceptable, and I strongly endorse an immediate nuclear freeze; at the same time, I reject abortion on demand. I want a radical change in US foreign policy toward the two-thirds world so that American influence sides with the poor masses rather than affluent elites and transnational corporations; but I also want much tougher laws against drunken driving to reduce murder on our highways. I believe women have been seriously oppressed, and I have endorsed the Equal Rights Amendment; but I also consider the strengthening of the family one of the most urgent concerns for current public policy and warmly approve President Reagan's attempt to have parents notified when public agencies give their minor children contraceptives.

As a resident of inner-city Philadelphia for a number of years, I protest the persisting gross inequality in education, housing, and jobs for Black, Hispanic, and other minorities; at the same time, I oppose the attempt of the homosexual and lesbian communities to use governmental processes to win social approval and legitimacy for their sexual lifestyles, although of course I defend the civil rights of homosexuals. I believe that we must protect the environment even though the result is slower economic growth; at the same time, I applaud citizens who use their economic roles to boycott companies whose advertising dollars support television programs crammed with sex and violence.

Some of the stances I take are identified with liberal/left movements, others with conservative/right causes. Now, it may be that I am simply a recalcitrant maverick or an inconsistent fool. But I hope not. I think there is reason in my madness. I have no commitment to ideologies of left or right. My only absolute commitment is to Jesus Christ. I am, of course, quite aware that our historical context conditions all our thinking. My goal, however, is to transcend ideological baggage and allow Jesus Christ and biblical revelation to be the decisive influence on the norms that shape my stand on all issues of public policy.

Nor am I alone in this. The civil rights and anti–Vietnam War movements helped a whole generation of younger evangelicals break free from their captivity to jingoistic nationalism and conservative ideology. Determined not to replace their former captivity to capitalist and right-wing ideologies with a new subservience to Marxism, they are rethinking their entire attitude toward public life from a radically biblical perspective. Magazines and organizations such as Sojourners, *The Other Side, Reformed Journal, Baptist Peacemaker*, the Association for Public Justice, and Evangelicals for Social Action are good examples.

Many of the most articulate faculty at the over one hundred evangelical colleges would have a similar outlook. In the evangelical seminaries (and almost all of the largest theological schools are evangelical today), a similar perspective is vigorously represented. Although it is impossible to give precise figures, younger evangelical social activists represent a significant and growing movement in America today.

The popular impression given by the media that Jerry Falwell speaks for the vast majority of evangelicals is simply incorrect. He may represent 15 to 25 percent of that large block of thirty to fifty million people that polls consistently identify as evangelical, but not more. According to a front-page story in the *New York Times* on Sunday, March 14, 1982, moderate evangelicals represent the mainstream of both current evangelicalism and Protestantism as a whole. Many in that mainstream majority and a growing minority that might prefer the label "radical evangelical" are committed to developing and articulating a new vision for American public life that grows out of the heart of historic biblical faith.

In the rest of my lecture, I want to state briefly why I believe we need a new vision for American public life; outline my methodology for moving from biblical faith to public policy; note a few presuppositions of my political philosophy; and, finally, articulate the kind of stand on specific issues that flows from that methodology.

The Need for a New Vision

No dominant vision or widely accepted ethical values undergird and shape public life today. Short-term economic or political self-interest rather than a common vision of justice and the common good determines most public decisions. The decay of traditional ethical values also profoundly affects the body politic as the family collapses and white-collar crime and corruption undermine business, law, medicine, and politics.

To the extent that there is an implicit guiding vision, it is a secular, materialistic one that virtually all religions would reject. I quote Bernard Zylstra, principal of the Institute for Christian Studies in Toronto:

> The expansion of the production of material goods, and their consumption, is the highest good, the summum bonum of twentieth-century civilization in Western Europe and North America. The increase in the gross national product (GNP) has become the chief end of human life, in comparison with which every other cultural purpose is secondary. The religion of production and consumption is the main cause of social disarray. For it permits the corporate industrial sector to encroach upon the legitimate social space of the family, marriage, education, the arts and the media. As a matter of fact, the very integrity of the state itself is endangered by the nearly uninhibited growth of the economic sector. The origin of this extremely one-sided cultural development must be found in a specific notion of human progress that gained preeminence since the time of the eighteenth-century Enlightenment. Simply stated, that notion holds that progress consists in the unlimited fulfillment of human material needs.[1]

Zylstra is correct in seeing the Enlightenment as a primary source for a number of contemporary problems. Abandoning the notion of a transcendent Creator who is the source of normative ethical values, the Enlightenment grounded ethics in autonomous humanity. The result has been two centuries of ethical relativism. First Marx, then Freud and the sociologists argued that ethical values are merely the product of sociocultural conditioning.

Modern science, or at least a pseudoscientific philosophy claiming the authority of science, has taught us that people are merely the product of a blind materialistic process governed by chance. In no way do I mean to deny that God the Creator used a long evolutionary process. But if all life is merely the product of random materialistic process, then persons are simply complex machines and ethical notions are mere subjective private feelings. The great mathematician and philosopher Bertrand Russell drew the proper conclusion: those who have the best poison gas, he said, will determine the ethics of the future. Ethics is what the momentarily powerful say is right. The Marxist claim that whatever serves the interests of the party is good and true is merely one of the more candid versions of the widespread ethical relativism rooted in the Enlightenment.

Radical evangelicals searching for a solid foundation for a new vision for American public life believe that in the last two centuries the Enlightenment's ethical relativism has been tested by Western society and found wanting. We also believe that the reasons were inadequate for abandoning the earlier Christian belief in a transcendent God who has intervened supernaturally in human history to reveal, among other things, ethical values that are an expression of God's very nature.

Right at the heart of the modern rejection of historic Christian theism and its understanding of ethics was the view that if one accepted the findings and implications of modern science, one could no longer believe in the supernatural elements of historic

Christianity. That meant that one would have to reject the heart of historic Christian theism because at its very center stood the two colossal miracles of the incarnation and resurrection.

Are the belief that God became flesh in a carpenter from Nazareth and the claim that Jesus was alive on the third day excluded by modern science? A host of philosophers and theologians from Hume and Kant to Ernst Troeltsch, Rudolph Bultmann, and Hans Küng have thought so. At the risk of seeming presumptuous, I want to argue that they were wrong. Certainly the critical historical investigation that emerged in the eighteenth and nineteenth centuries in conjunction with the growth of modern science helped us discover that many earlier miraculous tales were pure legend with no historical foundation. One can only be grateful for the more accurate historical knowledge that has emerged.

But it is sheer intellectual confusion to suppose that more and more scientific information makes belief in alleged miracles more and more intellectually irresponsible. Science simply tells us with greater and greater precision what nature regularly does. Or, to put it in Hume's terms, it simply describes observed regularity with greater and greater accuracy. In principle, no amount of scientific information could ever tell us whether there might or might not be a God who transcends the natural order of observed regularity. Of course, if an all-powerful being who transcends nature exists, then God can intervene in nature anytime God chooses.

Evangelical Christians believe that has happened in the history of Israel and the life of Jesus of Nazareth. If there were time, I would show why I as a historian think that the historical evidence for Jesus' life, death, and resurrection from the tomb is surprisingly strong. It was because of the resurrection that the early church confessed that at the name of Jesus, every knee shall bow and every tongue confess that he is Lord of the universe, true God as well as true man. It is because of the resurrection that I believe the same thing and therefore also accept Jesus' teaching as the very words of God. Jesus taught that the Old Testament was God's special revelation. The Christian church believes the same about the New Testament canon. Thus it is from God's Word as disclosed in the canon of the Old and New Testament that I want to develop the norms for a new vision for public life.

Methodology

Next, I turn to the question of methodology. How do I propose to move from the Bible to concrete public policy proposals?

One of the particularly valuable emphases of Bruce Birch's and Larry Rasmussen's excellent book, *Bible and Ethics in the Christian Life*, is the point that the Bible provides ethical guidance in a wide variety of ways. By focusing on two of these ways, I do not deny others. Two ways that the Bible provides the foundation for my vision for public life are (1) the biblical story supplies a basic perspective on all reality, and (2) the Bible provides normative paradigms for basic issues like the nature of economic justice.

1. First, the biblical story. From creation to consummation, the Bible portrays free, finite persons in dialogue with an infinite Creator. Made so they would be fulfilled only in free obedience to their Maker, persons have introduced enormous disorder into the entire created order through their proud attempt to place themselves rather than God at the center of reality.

Loving humanity too much to leave them alone in their self-destructive arrogance, God initiated a long redemptive process with Abraham and his descendants with the ultimate intention of restoring the broken beauty of creation to its original glory and wholeness. Repeatedly God intervened in special ways to disclose to God's chosen people an ever-broadening picture of the nature of shalom—a shalom that involves a complex web of right relationships between God and humans, persons and persons, and people and nature. When the covenant people constantly ignored God's invitation to shalom given through the law and the prophets, a faithful remnant began to look for a time in the future when the reign of God would break decisively into history with the coming of God's Messiah who would overcome all evil and usher in an eternal age of peace and justice.

Christians believe that ancient Jewish hope was fulfilled in an unexpected way in the person and work of the Carpenter from Nazareth. Claiming to be the Messiah sent to begin the messianic age, Jesus challenged every evil and injustice of the status quo. Repudiating the violent messianic hopes of his day, Jesus called his followers to love their enemies. Rejecting the sexual discrimination of his time, which excluded women from theological investigation and prohibited their appearing with men in public, Jesus treated women as equals. Ministering to the poor and oppressed and summoning his followers to do the same, Jesus challenged the economic establishment so thoroughly that they felt compelled to get rid of him. Rejecting the legalism of the religious leadership, he taught that God freely forgives even the worst of prodigals. He even claimed divine authority to forgive sinners. It is hardly surprising that he was crucified as a blasphemous heretic and dangerous social radical.

That would have been the end except that God raised Jesus from the dead on the third day. It was the resurrection that convinced the early Christians that Jesus' messianic claim was valid and that the long-expected messianic kingdom had genuinely broken into history. As a result, the early church imitated Jesus' sweeping challenge to the status quo by offering the world a radical new society incarnating Jesus' kingdom values on economic sharing, nonviolence, and the equality of all people. Women and slaves became persons. The rich engaged in costly economic sharing as there was need. And they loved their enemies even while burning at the stake. The very character of the early Christian community was tangible evidence that the messianic age of peace and justice expected by the prophets had already begun.

But it was also painfully clear that the old age of evil, injustice, and violence persisted, even to a certain degree, in the church. Jesus himself had taught that the expected kingdom of God was beginning in his life and work, but he had also said that the messianic kingdom of justice and peace would come in its fullness only at some time in the future. Christians therefore look forward to a coming day, known only to God, when the risen Christ will return to complete his victory over all evil and injustice, and God's people will live forever in the presence of the risen Lord.

This biblical story shapes the Christian approach to public life in profound ways. Persons are not merely complex machines to be programmed for the good of the state; they are immeasurably valuable beings so loved by their Creator that he suffered the hell of Roman crucifixion for them; free beings called to be co-shapers of history with God and neighbor; immortal beings whose ultimate destiny far transcends any passing political system. Public life is important because it shapes the social context in which persons respond to God's invitation to live in right relationship with God and neighbors. But the state is not ultimate, for it is accountable to the Creator of the galaxies who is the ultimate source of the true and the good.

2. The Bible as the source of normative paradigms. Next, I want to show how the Bible functions as the source of normative paradigms. Developing a biblical understanding of any issue (for instance, economic justice or the family) is not an easy, simple process. It is far more complex than selecting a few isolated proof texts related to a given topic.

If the entire biblical canon is God's Word, then one must carefully trace the treatment of a given issue throughout the entire development of biblical history, paying attention to the unique socioeconomic, historical context of each scriptural passage and carefully weighing the different emphases in all genres of biblical literature. Rigorous exegesis of each particular text, using the best biblical scholarship, is essential. Placing each passage within the broad sweep of biblical history is also important to understand the direction of development and the full complexity of the biblical revelation.

Let's assume someone wanted to develop a careful understanding of the biblical view of economic justice. That person would need to start with the stewardship of creation outlined in Genesis, proceed through the complex traditions about the land in the Pentateuch, carefully explore the prophetic denunciation of economic exploitation, examine the way Jesus' new messianic teaching and community fulfilled the prophetic hope for a new age of justice, probe the economic sharing in the early church, and understand the eschatological hope for a time when the tears and agony of the hungry and oppressed will be no more. Careful exegetical work would be necessary at every point.

But even after all the detailed exegesis had been done and one had developed a comprehensive, synthetic overview of the different, complementary perspectives on economic justice in all strands of biblical literature, the task would only have begun. Patriarchal society differed enormously from Roman Palestine, and both differ even more from the present global economy viewed from Wall Street, Tokyo, or Moscow. Any naive attempt to transplant this or that specific aspect of biblical economic life into the twentieth century ignores the vast differences between the past and the present. The biblical paradigm must be faithfully applied, not blindly copied. I quote from Chris Wright's forthcoming article on this problem in the first issue of the *International Journal of Christian Social Ethics* published by the World Evangelical Fellowship:

> It is assumed that cases and circumstances will differ, but if the principle is being properly applied, then it will be possible to recognize the pattern of the paradigm. In this sense, the social life

of Israel [and the early church]—their laws and institutions—are to be taken as paradigmatic. We know that our circumstances and context differ greatly from those of ancient Israel [and the early church]. But as we study them we are able to form objectives and policies and to initiate action in our day which recognizably displays the shape of the [biblical] paradigm.

To develop a specific concrete proposal for public policy today that is grounded in the biblical paradigm, one must combine (in either one person or, normally, a team of scholars) a thorough understanding of the Scriptures and a sophisticated understanding of contemporary society.

The most brilliant socioeconomic analyses would be indispensable, as would critical interaction with the methodology and the findings of the various schools in the social sciences. Pragmatic testing to see if the specific proposals work would also be important. But pervading the entire process would be fundamental biblical values. The concrete public policy proposals would be judged to be biblical if the contemporary proposals clearly reflected the shape of the biblical paradigm.

I believe that every area of American public life would profit enormously if a generation of evangelical biblical scholars, social scientists, politicians, businesspeople, and professionals in all fields engaged in these kinds of sweeping reexaminations of law, education, health care, the economy, and the political process. I am not so naive as to suppose that there would be complete agreement even among themselves. Christians cannot even agree on all the aspects of the biblical story. There would be more room for legitimate disagreement in the development of the biblical paradigms on the family, sexuality, economic justice, peace, the sacredness of human life, and so on. And when we arrived at specific public policy proposals developed to reflect the biblical paradigms, there would be still more room for honest disagreement among equally devout, equally competent, equally honest Christians.

This is the reason why the church qua church should not constantly make pronouncements on specific political options. The church should articulate the biblical story and the biblical paradigms. At times, a body of believers in a congregation or denomination will feel such clarity, agreement, and urgency that they will appropriately as church say what they believe the specific political applications of the biblical story and paradigms are. More often this will be done by individual Christians in public life and by interdenominational Christian associations (like Evangelicals for Social Action) whose specific purpose is the application of biblical data to the needs of current public policy. Such Christian associations and think tanks will always strive to develop clearly biblical proposals. They will always articulate clearly how they move from the normative biblical material to concrete contemporary proposals. But they will never claim divine authority for their specific suggestions. They will humbly assume that those who disagree with their specific proposals may also be faithful Christians. And they will hope that the ongoing dialogue will produce public policy proposals even more faithful to the biblical paradigms.

Before proceeding to sketch the social agenda that I believe would flow from the Scriptures, I need to make a few comments on some issues of my political philosophy that are at least consistent with, and I think follow from, the biblical material. I hardly need to add that here as elsewhere in this lecture I am covering vast territory in a brief span, and I am painfully aware that every issue demands far more comprehensive and sophisticated treatment.

Brief Comments toward a Political Philosophy

1. Separation of church and state. Lest you think that my agenda is beginning to sound like some theocratic attempt to use the state to impose evangelical Christianity on unwilling secular humanists, I want to reassure you that I do believe deeply in the separation of church and state. (I am, after all, a descendant of those sixteenth-century Anabaptists who died by the thousands as martyrs for this belief long before the rest of Western society accepted their radical proposal.) The state should not promote or establish any religion or denomination.

Nor is the separation of church and state merely a pragmatic necessity in a pluralistic society. Religious faith by its very nature is a free response to God. It cannot be coerced. Throughout biblical history, we see a sovereign God constantly inviting persons into free dialogue. God invites obedience but is astonishingly patient with those who decline the invitation. If the history of Israel tells us anything, it discloses how much space God gives people to reject God's will and still continue to enjoy the created gifts of food, health, and life. Jesus' parable of the wheat and tares (Matthew 13:24-30) makes it clear that God wants believers and nonbelievers to be able to live and enjoy the world together until the end of history. Since God intends history to be the place where people have the freedom to respond or not respond to God, the state should not promote or hinder religious belief.

Sometimes, however, the separation of church and state is confused with the separation of public life from ethical values grounded in religious faith. To charge, as columnists in the *New York Times* have, that the Rev. Jerry Falwell's political activity violates the separation of church and state is absurd. He is only doing what the National Council of Churches and Jewish organizations have done for decades. His political proposals may be unwise, but his proposing them hardly violates the separation of church and state.

Virtually every major political decision, virtually every debated public policy proposal, depends finally on basic value judgments that are rooted in religious belief. Our political stands, not just on abortion and the nuclear arms race, but also on US policy in Central America or the shape of the tax structure, depend in part finally on basic ethical commitments, whether conscious or unconscious. It would be as impossible as it would be immoral to try to separate public life from ethical values grounded in religious belief.

Every citizen is free to propose to the body politic a vision and a set of concrete public policy proposals for American society that grow out of his or her most basic religious beliefs. In a pluralistic democratic society, those proposals can become law only if a majority agrees. If, as Christians believe, biblical revelation represents God's truth about the world and persons, then public policy proposals made by Christians about economic justice or the family will often make sense and appeal to many citizens who do not share the religious foundations of those proposals.

I want to make one other brief comment on the separation of church and state. Probably the best protection against political totalitarianism is the recognition that the state is not the ultimate source of value and law. If people in a society believe strongly that a higher law grounded in God the Creator exists, to which current legislation ought to conform and which citizens ought to obey, even if that means civil disobedience, totalitarianism will be held in check. But how can a secular state that is neutral toward religious conviction recognize the fact that governmental activity and law are finally accountable to God? In the US, we have done it with things like congressional chaplains, coins engraved with the slogan "In God We Trust," and, for a long time, prayer in the public schools. But all of these are inconsistent with the separation of church and state.

I believe that the responsibility for articulating this important protection against totalitarianism must be carried not by the state, but by religious bodies and religious individuals in politics. Large numbers of devout politicians inculcated by their churches and synagogues with a deep awareness that they are finally accountable to God will be a far better way to preserve the societal understanding, than will inscriptions on coins, that the state is not ultimate. There is no reason why presidents and congressional leaders cannot frequently express publicly their personal conviction that no government is absolute and that the state's actions ought to conform to the norms and values grounded in the Creator. Frequent personal, albeit public, acknowledgment of this conviction would not violate the separation of church and state, while at the same time it would promote general acceptance of a crucial idea.

2. *Decentralized and global government.* Next, a brief comment about both decentralized and global government. The reasons for decentralized government are both positive and negative. Positively, biblical faith sees persons and families called to be co-shapers of history, responsible agents free to help shape the things that affect their lives. The more decentralized decision-making is, the more this is possible.

Negatively, the doctrine of human sin which explains the dictum that power tends to corrupt and absolute power corrupts absolutely warns us not to centralize power. Decentralized decision-making, then, even if that means a certain loss of efficiency, is in keeping with the biblical doctrine of sin and the biblical vision of persons as co-shapers under God of their own history.

On the other hand, biblical faith also contains a powerful global thrust. The one Sovereign of the entire universe has created all persons equal and cares equally about the total well-being of every person. The selfish nationalism and narrow patriotism of modern nation-states find no justification in biblical thought. Therefore, Christians should strengthen global institutions like the United Nations, but they should do so in such a way that decision-making always occurs at as local a level as is consistent with the demands of justice, order, and freedom.

3. *The importance of intermediate associations.* Third, a comment on the importance of intermediate associations. In the biblical paradigms of the state and the family, the individual is not

46

nearly as absolute as in the dominant American political philosophy that goes back to John Locke. Historian Rockne McCarthy, a member of a Christian political organization called the Association for Public Justice, puts it this way:

> The Enlightenment produced a liberal (individualist) tradition in which the rights of sovereign individuals are absolutized. This atomistic view of the sovereign individual became . . . a master assumption of American political thought. John Locke is recognized as the philosophical founder of the American liberal tradition. In his view of social reality, individuals are sovereign, and, therefore, inherently free of every associational relationship. From such a perspective all social entities are mere abstractions. Thus only individuals have rights because only individuals are "real."[2]

This sovereignty of the individual can be seen in recent legal decisions that make the mother the sole determinant of whether the offspring of a husband and wife should be aborted and deny that parents must be informed when their teenagers receive contraceptives.

A biblical perspective would pay far more attention to the fact that individuals are members of intermediate associations (such as the family and the church or synagogue) that also have rights and responsibilities that the state should recognize and preserve. The biblical paradigm of the family would suggest that both husband and wife have a crucial stake in the decision about abortion (if indeed abortion is allowed). Similarly, the right of parents to know about and exercise responsibility for the fact that their minor teenagers are receiving contraceptives overrides other valid concerns.

4. *What ethical values should be legislated?* My final comment in this section on political philosophy deals with the question of what ethical values should be legislated and what should not?

From the perspective of biblical faith, adultery and racism in the rental of housing are equally sinful. Does that mean that there should be laws against both? If not, why not?

I argue that the state should not legislate criminal penalties for breaking biblical ethical norms except where those infractions violate the rights of others. The churches, of course, should have their own internal mechanisms for dealing with lying, adultery, racist attitudes, and so on. Therefore, laws against racial prejudice in the sale or rental of housing to guarantee that the rights of others are not violated are appropriate, whereas laws making adultery a civil offense are not.

Obviously, this general principle does not solve all problems. Alcoholic mothers or fathers and adulterous spouses harm their families as well as themselves. That injury, however, extends to a relatively small number of people who have a special commitment to each other. Racial discrimination in housing, on the other hand, affects a whole class of people indiscriminately.

The very nature of the family entails implied consent that all members share both the positive and the negative aspects of family life. This mutual commitment and the family's existence as an intermediate association independent of the state means that the state should not intervene in the family except in extreme situations like serious physical abuse of spouse or children or denial of medical treatment necessary for survival. Thus, citizens should be free to break accepted (e.g., biblical) ethical norms without legal penalty except where such infractions violate the rights of others.

The fact that the state does not legally prohibit adultery or homosexuality or divorce, however, does not mean that it cannot offer incentives for a lifestyle or ethical stance that it considers helpful for society. The state could appropriately through its tax laws make marriage more advantageous financially than cohabitation.

Thus far I have pointed to the need and source for a new vision for American public life, outlined my methodology for moving from the Bible to public policy, and then made a few observations on my political philosophy. Now I turn to my fourth and last section—an overview of the kind of public policy that I believe would faithfully reflect biblical paradigms.

Limitations of both time and expertise, unfortunately, prevent my developing in detail the methodology I have outlined on even one issue. Instead, I shall take a few key issues of particular importance and sketch some aspects of the relevant biblical paradigms and then suggest the general direction that public policy should go. Vastly more work by both biblical scholars and social scientists is obviously imperative.

Some Proposals for Public Policy

First a comment about what I call biblical balance. If Christians want to help shape public policy in ways that are faithful to the Scriptures, then they must reject one-issue politics and search for a political agenda that reflects the balance of biblical concerns. Since justice for the poor is one of the most central themes in the Bible, it is flatly unbiblical for someone like Rev. Jerry Falwell to develop Moral Majority and fail to make justice for the poor central to his political agenda. Certainly the Bible also reflects a profound concern for the family and the sacredness of human life. But surely justice for the poor must be one central concern of any evangelical political program. Only if the full range of our political concerns reflects the emphases of the Scriptures can Christians claim to have a biblically shaped political agenda.

In this section, therefore, I deal both with issues of great concern to liberal activists (e.g., issues of economic justice and global peace), and also with issues rightly emphasized by conservatives (e.g., the family and the sacredness of human life).

1. Economic justice. The starting point of all biblical thinking on economics is that Yahweh is sovereign. God alone is the only absolute owner of all things, and God intends the earth's resources to be used for the benefit of all.

The Bible rejects all notions of absolute private ownership of property. As a passage like the Jubilee text in Leviticus 25 indicates, the right of families to have the resources to earn their own way is a higher right than the property rights of the person who has purchased land. That is not to deny all notions of private ownership. Limited private ownership of property understood as stewardship of resources for the good of family and neighbor in obedience to God the ultimate owner is the biblical pattern. Centralizing all economic power in the state through state ownership of all means of production does not correspond to the biblical paradigm and almost guarantees totalitarianism.

Great extremes of wealth and poverty are displeasing to the God revealed in the Bible. The Old Testament contains institutionalized structures (rather than mere charity) that, if followed, would have systematically prevented or reduced a huge gap between rich and poor. Although they do not suggest a wooden, legalistic equality of consumption, the biblical patterns of economic sharing in both testaments move in the opposite direction from great economic inequality. Probably nothing is clearer in the Scriptures than God's special concern for and identification with the poor, weak, and oppressed.

I am a theologian, not a political scientist or economist, so I will not try to suggest a detailed economic program and a political strategy for implementing the biblical paradigm. But I do want to suggest the general direction that I believe is required. Economic injustice for the poor both here and abroad should become a top concern in American politics. It is intolerable to make the poorer sections of American society pay the social costs of reducing inflation. A fundamental redistribution of power and resources (including education, productive capabilities, and capital) is necessary within the United States.

Internationally, a fundamentally different US foreign policy is essential. The Scriptures totally reject any idea of private ownership that suggests that Americans have a right to enjoy for themselves all the natural resources and abundance that our particular geography and history place in our hands. Even if it is costly, even if it would lower our standard of living, the first priority of US foreign policy toward the two-thirds world should be the elimination of hunger and poverty and the promotion of programs that enable the poorest one-half of the world's people to earn their own way.

2. *The family.* In the biblical paradigm, the family is one of the central divinely willed intermediate societal associations. Lifelong marital covenant between one man and one woman is the Christian norm. The family, not the state, is the primary institution for rearing children. Christians must resist the growing tendency of the state to usurp the role of the family.

That the contemporary family is in trouble is generally acknowledged. Primary responsibility for revitalizing and renewing the biblical vision of the family and sexuality lies, of course, not with the state and the media but with religious institutions. But state and media do have a significant secondary role. Surely it is not too much to ask that TV, radio, and film portray far more often than they currently do models of wholesome families and sexual fidelity. If the only artistically excellent scripts that arrive on the desks of the elite who control the content of the media always portray sexual promiscuity and broken homes, then that small circle of artists and producers needs to be expanded.

Economic pressure on advertisers via consumer boycotts is one way to begin. All legislation, including tax structures, should help create a social and financial climate conducive to strong, responsible families and lifelong marriage covenant. Parents, not the state, have the responsibility for helping teenagers avoid pregnancy.

Evangelicals for Social Action has commissioned a public policy task force to explore ways that governmental policy (including the welfare system) with reference to low-income persons could be changed to strengthen the family among the poor. A similar task force will soon be commissioned to ask how a new view of public and private initiatives could strengthen the family in all segments of society. Vastly more needs to be done by Christian organizations and think tanks in order that the American public can be given some clear public policy options for government and media that would strengthen rather than further weaken the family.

3. The sacredness of human life. Every person is created in the image of God. Since God desires all to be saved so much that God sent his Son to die "as a ransom for all people" (1 Timothy 2:4, 6, NIV), every person in the world is immeasurably valuable. The value and worth of each person are totally independent of their social usefulness or their ability to experience a certain standard of self-fulfillment. A host of difficult issues, including euthanasia and genetic engineering, demands attention in this section. But I have time for only one of the most difficult and most controversial issues—namely, abortion. I believe the Supreme Court decision in 1973 was a fundamental mistake that must be corrected, if necessary, by constitutional amendment.

Developments in the last ten years already provide some indication of the dangerous road that may lead from abortion to scientific experimentation on fetuses, which will lead to late-term abortions, killing of the deformed, and infanticide. At the very least, we must reject abortion as a convenient method of birth control and permit it only in the cases of rape, incest, or danger to the physical life of the mother. My own position is that we should decide as a society that before the law the fetus is a person from the time of conception and therefore that abortion is permissible only if the physical life of the mother is in danger. Biologically, the fetus is obviously human life. Since there is no explicit biblical teaching on whether or when the fetus is a human being, it is better to err on the side of caution.

I am aware of the problems of this position. But I believe it presents fewer difficulties and dangers than the alternatives. Certainly, Christians who adopt this stance must actively support pregnancy centers and adoption programs for unmarried women (especially teenagers) who become pregnant. It is to the credit of the Christian Action Council, the major evangelical anti-abortion lobby, that they have done this in a major way.

4. *Peacemaking in a nuclear age.* Finally, the nuclear arms race and my most radical proposals. Most Christians stand within the just war tradition. I have argued elsewhere that if one applies the criteria of the just war tradition to the question of nuclear weapons, the appropriate conclusion is that one must reject not only the use of strategic nuclear weapons (and also tactical nuclear weapons, since their use would probably escalate to strategic weapons) but also their very possession. That was the recent conclusion of the vast majority of Christian leaders from all parts of the world who met in Sweden from April 20 to 24, 1983. If we were correct, then Christians must demand not only an immediate freeze on all testing and deployment, but also total nuclear disarmament within some short, specified time.

In fact, I think we need to go even further. Christians must be prepared to act according to our own ethical tradition regardless of what the Soviet Union does. If we argue that we will even commit what the just war tradition says is murder to protect ourselves from Soviet totalitarianism, then the ethical relativism of Marxist thought has already conquered. If the possession of nuclear weapons is immoral, then we must abandon them no matter what the Kremlin does.

But this stance does not require unilateral disarmament. I believe we should be ready to die to defend democratic freedom, although I do not believe we should murder hundreds of millions of people to protect ourselves against Soviet totalitarianism. I think we should seriously explore the possibility of what Gene Sharp and others call civilian-based defense as an alternative national policy for defending democratic values. In the last section of our book *Nuclear Holocaust and Christian Hope*, Dick Taylor and I have spelled out how the tactics of Gandhi and Martin Luther King Jr. could be adopted by a total society for national self-defense. I know such a proposal sounds politically naive. But the only alternatives, if we cannot negotiate bilateral disarmament, are unilateral disarmament or nuclear holocaust.

For centuries humanity has sought security through violence. Almost all societies have hoped that state-of-the-art weapons would deter aggressive neighbors. Sometimes it worked for short intervals, but seldom for long.

Ever more sophisticated technology provided ever more deadly weapons. Clubs gave way to longbows, chariots to tanks, and cannons to nuclear missiles and lasers. Very seldom, and never for long did the new weapons improve anyone's security. Even more deadly weapons merely guaranteed that the next battle would destroy even more people.

Today we stand at the end of that long violent road littered with the mangled bodies of our best sons and daughters. Today state-of-the-art weapons enable us to destroy the planet. Every new generation of nuclear weapons shortens the nuclear trigger and reduces our security. The wisest insight of conventional wisdom is suicidal madness. We are at an impasse.

The only way to avoid disaster is to take a different path. Security through violence has never worked well; it will not work at all today. Martin Luther King was right: "Today the choice is no longer between violence and nonviolence. It is either nonviolence or nonexistence."[3]

For the first three centuries, the early Christians rejected the violence of war as well as of abortion and capital punishment. They did so because they believed that Jesus' summons to love their enemies was a daring call to reject lethal violence as the way to security and peace. I believe Jesus' costly invitation to suffer rather than kill is the only alternative to the path that leads to nuclear holocaust. If American society would try it, we would undoubtedly pay a heavy price, but we would also lead the way out of the impasse that ends in global suicide.

I am quite aware that my proposal for civilian-based defense sounds incredibly naive in the realistic world of power politics so brilliantly described by people like Henry Kissinger. But brilliant realism and the wisdom of power politics have brought us to the brink of annihilation. Is it not time to seriously consider an alternative?

To survive, American public life requires radical transformation. I am quite aware that my proposals will not become accepted political policy in 1984 or 1988. Since the major political parties are parties of consensus, fundamentally new political ideas, as American history shows, must initially find a home outside the major political parties. That is happening today in a significant segment of the Christian church.

In his brilliant Harvard doctoral dissertation "Revivalism and Social Reform," historian Timothy Smith showed how the American tradition of religious revivals played a major role in the development of the abolitionist movement against slavery. More and more evangelicals are beginning to talk about a similar movement today.

We dream about a peace revival sweeping the American churches. We dream of millions of people experiencing or returning to a vivid personal relationship with God in Christ. We dream of millions of Christians discovering the biblical God of shalom, the God who invites the people of our unjust, polluted, and endangered planet to return to right relationships with the Creator, other persons, and nature. We dream of a vast movement of Christians so captivated by the biblical vision of shalom that they join other persons of goodwill in our pluralistic society in a sustained campaign for economic justice, stable families, an end to racial and sexual discrimination, the protection of the environment and the sacredness of human life, and global peace. I expect to see some major part of my vision for American public life become a reality only if the Sovereign of history astonishes our secular society with a mighty peace revival.

Even then, of course, we would not have utopia. Politicians and preachers would still often be petty, selfish, and misguided. Societal institutions would still need restructuring. But we might at least wend our way through the next two most dangerous decades in human history without experiencing global disaster. That itself would be enough. That itself would be enough to confirm my belief that the best clue about the nature of reality is contained in the biblical story about the God of shalom who became flesh in the Peacemaker from Nazareth.

Notes

1. Quoted in Mark Hatfield, *Confessing Christ and Doing Politics*, ed. James Skillen (Washington, DC: Center for Public Justice), 1982, 52–55.

2. Quoted in Hatfield, 66–67.

3. Quoted from the "I've Been to the Mountaintop" speech by Martin Luther King Jr., to the sanitation workers at Mason Temple, Memphis, TN, April 3, 1968.

CHAPTER 4

Building a Christian Social Movement

This is a keynote speech initially given on October 26, 1985, at a conference sponsored by Evangelicals for Social Action (ESA) in Washington, DC. I presented a version of this speech over three dozen times in the next decade in the United States, Canada, Australia, New Zealand, and South Korea. The speech was given at a time when ESA, which I led, was flourishing even though it had existed as a membership organization for only seven years. I wanted to sketch a vision of how ESA should proceed and what principles should guide us.

The year 1985, the middle of the Reagan presidency, was a period of harsh political disagreement. (It was probably the time of the most severe attacks on me personally.) My goal was to propose ways to talk openly and honestly across different political sectors. Obviously that problem has not only not improved but has grown immensely more serious in the intervening decades.

My basic proposal was to make a commitment to Jesus Christ and God's revelation in the Bible our central guide. Back then I thought biblical balance was central, and I still do—as my 2018 commencement address at Biblical Seminary in Hatfield, Pennsylvania, "Biblical Balance, Biblical Balance," chapter 17, demonstrates.

Over Thanksgiving weekend in 1973 about forty evangelicals gathered together in the YMCA in Chicago to talk about social ethics. The result was the Chicago Declaration of Evangelical Social Concern. Back then, such a meeting was sufficiently unusual that a major newspaperwoman said that perhaps our gathering was the most significant church-related event of 1973. Evangelicals did not get together very often to talk about social ethics in that day.

Today these gatherings happen frequently. No longer is the primary question whether biblical Christians should be dealing with social ethics, with public policy, with peace, justice, and liberty. Rather, it is what the shape of a biblical response to these issues should be. Growing out of the Chicago Declaration, Evangelicals for Social Action (ESA) has felt led by God to try to develop a biblical response to the issues of public policy. God is doing something very special in ESA, and I am incredibly grateful. This weekend underlines that and renews the courage and the commitment and the excitement of all of us who have been at it for a long time. You don't know how much you are encouraging us by just being here from all over the country.

I would like to share one story to illustrate and underline that. I talked to a sister today who said that she grew up in a non-Christian home. She was a Marxist. She was converted a little more than five years ago, came to Christ, and gave up her commitment to violence and Marxism. But she was converted in a context where there wasn't much concern about justice and peace. In fact, some thought her concerns in those areas verged on the demonic. And for five years she squelched that part of herself. Then about six months ago, God sent ESA her way. And today she is working with our president, Dr. Vernon Grounds, and others, trying to form a chapter in Boulder. That is what ESA is about; that is what God is trying to do through us.

What we are trying to do is build a Christian social justice, peace, and liberty movement in the late 1980s. That is what I want to talk about. How do we do that?

I could answer the question in one sentence. It is really all very simple. We simply maintain a biblical balance. I could stop there. I am told that Winston Churchill went back to his old school (I think it was Harrow) and gave a speech. It consisted of this: "Never give in! Never give in! Never, never, never, never, never, never." Then he sat down. I am not going to do that. Sorry.

Another way to say it is to say that I am not committed finally to anything except Jesus Christ and his kingdom. I am not committed to social justice, to nuclear disarmament, to a pro-life agenda, or to the family. I have absolutely no commitment to ideologies of left or right; I am not committed to anything except Jesus Christ and biblical revelation. I want to submit every part of my life to the lordship of Christ. That does not mean that when we make that our goal, we manage it perfectly. It is a long process; it takes a lifetime. But that is what we are about, and I think that is what you are about. And when we do that, then Christ sends us back to the Scriptures for biblical balance. And that means (and this is what I want to talk about) both evangelism and social responsibility. It means both inward journey and outward journey. It means both inward body life in the local congregation and outward mission in the social order. It means both personal and corporate concerns. It means both sensitive person-centered spirits and courageous revelation-centered stands. It means both biblical analysis and social analysis. It means both justice and freedom, both peace and the sanctity of life, because we are committed to a biblically balanced agenda. And it means, finally, both love and truth in debate. Briefly, I'd like to address each of those things.

Evangelism and social responsibility. Almost a hundred years ago now, there was a very major movement of concern for justice in the church, especially in the American church. And it became dreadfully one-sided. It lost a concern for biblical orthodoxy and evangelism. There is a possibility that you and I could repeat that mistake in the '80s and '90s. We don't need to, and I don't think we will. But we need to resolve, with all of our hearts, to make sure that we don't. We need to decide that we will be committed to both.

I think there are a lot of ways to work at that. It doesn't mean, of course, that every organization has the same vocation and agenda. ESA is not an evangelistic organization. We are not trying to compete with the Billy Graham Evangelistic Association. We are focused on public policy. But as an organization, we say that evangelism is every bit as crucial and every bit as important as our concern. And we need to work at that in a lot of ways. I wish that the Lord would lead some of us to reverse roles in some ways. I think it is absolutely fantastic that Jim Wallis is sensing a call to lead peace revivals around the country. We need to pray for him. In our individual lives, I think we need to ask God to give us the gift of evangelism. We need to constantly insist as individuals in ESA that one is as important as the other. As a movement we need to covenant before God to maintain that biblical balance.

Inward journey and outward journey. Second, we need both an inward journey and an outward journey. Richard Lovelace (our board member), who is home sick this weekend, has said that most of those who are praying are not praying for peace and justice, and most of those who are working for peace and justice are not praying. That is not entirely true. Praise God, it is increasingly less true. But there is enough truth in it to make us all uncomfortable.

The inward journey of prayer and dependence on the Spirit needs to be a crucial part of our movement. Andrew Murray, in his classic *With Christ in the School of Prayer*, says that in prayer we change history, that in prayer we hold the hand of the hand that holds the destiny of the universe. Jesus promised us, "If you remain in me and my words remain in you, ask whatever you wish, and it will be done for you" (John 15:7, NIV). For a long time, I did not fully believe that. But increasingly, I feel that it is a little outrageous not to believe what God in the flesh said. And slowly, my faith is growing. Prayer should be just as central to Evangelicals for Social Action as it is to the Billy Graham Evangelistic Association. In our ESA board meetings, we try to implement that in practical ways. We take an issue, put it on the table and see what we are talking about, and then we stop and pray and ask that God will guide us on that issue. I hope that every local chapter is a praying chapter, a chapter where prayer chains happen on occasion. A chapter where there are weekend retreats on spiritual renewal as well as vigorous action.

A few years ago, in 1980, I had the privilege of being in England and spent a weekend with David Watson. Some of you knew him. He was a tremendous evangelist in the Anglican Church in England, one of the wonderful charismatic leaders of our generation. I must confess that I rather hoped that something very dramatic would happen on that weekend, that perhaps I would start speaking in tongues. I didn't, although I would not have objected at all. It was rather ordinary in that regard. As a matter of fact, I don't happen to speak in tongues, so relax, if that would worry you. Toward the end of our time together, David Watson said to me, "Ron, I have prayed daily for many, many years for the gift of Spirit-filled evangelism, and the Lord has answered that prayer in tremendous ways." And that is certainly true. He was used of God in fantastic ways to bring thousands of people to personal faith in Christ. And then he said, "I hear the Spirit saying to me that you should pray regularly for the gift of Spirit-filled work for peace and justice." And I have taken that as a word from the Lord. I try to do that regularly. And I would like to give that invitation to you. I wish every person in ESA would pray regularly to God for the gift of Spirit-filled work for peace, for justice, for

61

liberty. 1 wouldn't be surprised if God wants to do signs and wonders in Evangelicals for Social Action's work for public justice just as much as God does signs and wonders on occasion in other kinds of ministry. ESA will be no stronger than the inward life of prayer and dependence on the Spirit of each of you and all the rest of us around the country.

Now, of course, prayer is no substitute for action. You know I am an activist and I want to change public policy. That is right; we need to do that. But our activism needs to be grounded in a deep life of dependence on God through prayer and study of the Scriptures. Both the inward journey and the outward journey are essential.

Inward body life and outward mission. Third, a successful movement in our time must have both inward body life in the local congregation and outward mission in the social order. I like the way Tom Skinner puts it. He says the church is supposed to be a little picture now of what heaven will be like.

I think that one of the weaknesses of mainline social action in the '60s was that too often the folk who went to Washington to lobby for legislation were generals without troops, as Senator Hatfield has said. They didn't represent local congregations who were already beginning to model what they were talking about. It's a farce, finally, to ask Washington to legislate what Christians will not live. If I am not beginning to allow the Holy Spirit to work out whatever pain, tension, and conflict may exist in my marriage with Arbutus, then it is a farce for me to suppose that I know how to tell President Reagan to work out reconciliation in the international political community. If I am not beginning to allow the Holy Spirit to restore and renew my local congregation so that we begin to model the shalom that we are pleading for in the larger society, it doesn't make a lot of sense to go to Washington. Now, I am not saying that we have to have perfect congregations or perfect marriages before we engage in political action. But we need to be on the way in our personal lives and in our churches. As we plunge into social change, we need to keep stressing the importance of body life. But, again, body life by itself can be merely narcissism. Christ gave his life for the world, and so should you and so should each of our congregations. Both inward body life in the congregation and outward mission to the social order are essential.

Personal and corporate concerns. Fourth, we need both personal and corporate concerns. I want to focus that on two specific areas. First of all, personal sin and corporate sin. I think Evangelicals for Social Action has done a pretty good job of raising up and focusing the important biblical teaching that the structures themselves can also be unjust and displeasing to God. We have pointed out in our tracts, for instance, that Amos said, "For three sins of Judah, even for four, I will not relent" (Amos 2:4, NIV). And he goes on to tell about the ways Israel was oppressing and trampling on the poor. That is very important and very significant. But we have also from the beginning of ESA not forgotten that that verse continues and says that God is going to punish them not only because of their economic oppression of the poor but also because of their sexual sin. Not always have social activists insisted on that balance. There have been sad public cases where it has not been the case. You know, Satan is a wretch. I hate him more year by year. Satan will destroy us and our ministries in any way he can. And sex is one good way to do it.

Divorce and sexual infidelity create enormous pain in our society today. In my book *Rich Christians in an Age of Hunger*, in the section where I dealt with social sin and personal sin, I ended the first edition with the words "Social sin is just as wrong as personal sin, and it is more subtle and it hurts more people." I changed that in the second edition. I still said the first two things, but I dropped the suggestion that it hurts more people. That may be true in the third world; I am not sure. But in North America there is so much pain and hell because of unfaithfulness in our personal lives, especially in the family, that I feel personal sin is equally devastating. We need to keep a balance in ESA and insist that both are important because the Bible says so. And also because, as we look around, we can see that it is true.

The second area where we stress both personal and corporate concerns is ministering to victims and changing the social structures that produce those victims. It is very important and very significant, and I praise God for local chapters who are getting involved in direct ministry to individual human needs. But the genius of ESA is to take that concern that is in our churches around the country, that concern for victims, and use it to help people see that there are reasons why victims are created. If we don't go on and help them see that, then we may merely support an unjust situation by picking up victims and not helping them to understand the underlying causes.

I heard an Indian bishop speak in India a few years back, and he was underlining the importance of getting to the source, the structural source, of problems. He told a story to underline that point. He said there was once an insane asylum that had a very simple way of finding out if people who were there had developed to a point where it was no longer necessary for them to stay. He said they would take the person to a large tub of water, turn on the tap, fill up the tub, leave the tap running, and then give the person a spoon and tell them to empty the tub. If the person started dipping the water out of the tub and did not turn off the tap, they knew the person was still crazy.

Sometimes we approach social problems in that way. We fail to go to the root of the problem. We deal with victims one spoonful at a time. In Sri Lanka when they sprayed the marshes where the mosquitoes that spread malaria bred, they cut back the death rate in three years by as much as Western Europe had cut back its death rate in three hundred years. That was a structural change of public health through preventative medicine. I would submit that that structural approach is more spiritual than either praying for the sick or building hospitals. I believe with all of my heart in doing both of those things. I believe God heals the sick. But we need to get to the root of structural problems.

There is a radical difference between using ministries of service to victims to lead people into structural understanding and structural change on the one hand, and on the other hand merely sticking to relief. You know that the most repressive leaders in the world are glad to affirm relief. A book was written by a fairly prominent evangelical on the issue of world hunger sometime back. It was dedicated to the Christian leaders Mr. and Mrs. Thieu in Vietnam and Mr. and Mrs. Somosa of Nicaragua. Tragically, both leaders promoted and benefited from oppressive, unjust systems.

Comfortable, affluent American society does not want to hear the truth about structural injustice. We fail God if we do not pay the cost of speaking that truth. As we do that, of course, it is absolutely crucial that we get our facts straight, that we speak the prophetic word with tears and with love. But we must speak that truth.

There must be a personal and a corporate dimension to our concern both at the level of our understanding of sin and also at the level of our solutions.

Person-centered spirit and courageous, revelation-centered stand. Fifth, we need both a person-centered spirit and a courageous revelation-centered stand. It is possible to be rigid, to be unconcerned with people, to neglect love. That is a real danger and an awful thing when it happens. To be so concerned with our structures or our ideologies or even our theologies that we trample on people and are unconcerned and hurt them is sin. But I think the greater danger, in our time, lies somewhere else.

I think the greater danger lies in a radical relativism: "I'm okay, you're okay." Whatever feels good to you is fine for you, and whatever feels good for me is fine for me. And don't dare be so outrageous and medieval and un-American as to suggest that there is some norm that I ought to follow even if it doesn't feel right to me. I think that that fundamental relativism in our society is devastating. It is seeping into evangelical life and thought and practice. I'm not sure that it is even doing it slowly; it is moving fast.

I want to illustrate it with the difficult, painful area of homosexuality. Evangelicals must confess that we have been dreadfully rigid, harsh, unloving, homophobic. We have not loved and accepted homosexuals. God forgive us for those times when our harshness has pushed people away from Christ. But we dare not simply submit to modern trends, to the next liberation movement that comes down the pike. The Bible is our norm, and the Bible is rather clear. Certainly there is a distinction between homosexual orientation and practicing homosexuality. But practicing it, the Bible clearly says, is wrong. We need to stand on that rock. But we need to do it with a sensitive, person-centered spirit. We need to love and cry and weep and support those who struggle. We need both a sensitive, person-centered spirit and a courageous, revelation-centered stand.

Biblical analysis and social analysis. Sixth, we need both biblical analysis and social analysis. Karl Barth said that Christians ought to take the newspaper in one hand and the Bible in the other. That is the way ESA tries to approach social issues. It is absolutely essential to start with the Bible. Otherwise, our work to change public life is merely ideological bias, and it ends up being absolutely useless. The last thing we need is more people reinforcing the status quo. But that is what we do unless we have some perspective that transcends the mistakes and failures of our own society. That is precisely, of course, what the biblical perspective gives us. If we stand on God's truth, we have that transcendent perspective.

There is a deep need today for a movement of Christians that transcends left and right and the mediocre middle, and rethinks every area of life from the biblical perspective. Now, that is not easy to do. It is very tough at a number of levels. It is not just a matter of collecting a number of proof texts and then thinking you have it. If the whole Bible is our canon, and that is what we believe, then we need to listen to every part of the Bible. We need to listen to every strand of biblical material if we are interested in a biblical perspective on a given issue. We need to do careful biblical scholarship at all of those points.

Let us assume, as ESA does, that we want to develop a careful understanding of the biblical view of economic justice. Well, we need to start with the stewardship of creation outlined in Genesis. We need to proceed through the complex traditions about the land in the first five books in the Old Testament. We need to explore carefully the prophetic denunciation of economic exploitation. We need to examine Jesus' new messianic teaching on community and sharing with the poor. We need to probe the economic sharing in the early church. We need to understand, finally, the eschatological hope for a time when, at Christ's return, the tears and the agony of the hungry and oppressed will be no more. Careful exegesis is important at all of those points.

Even then the task would only be half done. The Bible does not give us a detailed blueprint on how to change the complex, modern economic world. We have to develop a synthetic overview of what the Bible says about a given area, and then we need to apply it to our complex modern world. We must *apply* the biblical paradigm. That involves careful social analysis after we have done our biblical homework. It requires a very sophisticated knowledge of the modern world. It requires the social sciences. We need to take the biblical principles, the biblical paradigms, the biblical norms, and apply them in our complex world.

Just knowing that God is on the side of justice for the poor doesn't tell you the best way to reform the welfare system today. Or the best way—is it foreign aid or private investment or neither?—

to empower poor folk in poor nations to stand on their own feet and earn their own way. It requires brilliant scholarship using the best socioeconomic analysis.

Evangelicals for Social Action tries within its modest means to combine those things. Certainly, we are only on the way. If somebody would give us ten million dollars, we would move faster. We ought to have a major evangelical think tank working on this. ESA would love to have a half dozen issues analysts working on those things. If ESA is to develop the way we want it to, it needs a sophisticated capability for public policy analysis.

I know all of this seems complicated. Believe me, I am not saying that before any of you do anything more in the area of peace, justice, and liberty, you must do three years of sophisticated biblical study and then three more years of economic and social analysis. We can start where we are and begin to apply what we know in modest ways. We can read the Scriptures for ourselves, we can read the newspapers regularly, and we can begin, knowing that even though our analysis at both levels is imperfect, God will use us and forgive us where we make mistakes. As we proceed, we will learn more. But we need that kind of sophisticated capability. We need organizations that have that ability. That is why we need each other in ESA. We need both careful biblical analysis and sophisticated social analysis.

Biblically balanced agenda. Seventh, we need a biblically balanced agenda. We care about both justice and freedom, about both family and economic justice, about both the sacredness of human life and nuclear disarmament. One-issue politics is dangerous for the body politic as well as unbiblical.

If Christians with political power want to make any claim that Christ is Lord of their political lives, then they must adopt a political agenda that reflects the balance of biblical concerns. I would submit that that is the best test of whether anybody's political agenda is shaped by ideological bias or by the Scriptures. If the

Scriptures repeatedly tell us that God is very concerned about justice for the poor, then it is fundamentally (i.e., biblically) unacceptable for Christians to start Moral Majority and decide—as Jerry Falwell admitted in an interview a few years ago in *Christianity Today*—that justice for the poor will not be a major item of concern. If the Scriptures tell us that human life is almost infinitely precious and that the family is a central, divinely willed intermediate institution in society, then it is fundamentally unacceptable to endorse a political platform that ignores or weakens societal concern for life and for family. And if biblical faith emphasizes the importance of both freedom and justice, it will not do to support institutions and trends that sacrifice one to the other. It is ironic that some of the same people who rightly charge ecumenical church leaders with stressing justice and forgetting about freedom so often produce programs that do the reverse. They sacrifice justice for the sake of freedom.

It is essential to keep our eyes on the North Star of biblical balance lest we lurch from one extreme to another. We also need to remember that Jesus and the prophets were usually challenging and resisting cultural trends rather than conforming to the dominant consensus. If one is radical in the '60s and neoconservative in the '80s, we ought to ask who is setting the agenda in both the '60s and the '80s. If the family is a biblical concern, it should have been a concern in the '60s. And if it wasn't, we ought to repent of that. And if justice for the poor was a biblical imperative in the '60s, then it ought to be central to any faithful Christian political movement in the '80s. In fact, precisely at a time when the larger American society seems to want to ignore the poor both at home and abroad, Christians will stubbornly insist on a biblical vision that places great emphasis on that point without thereby neglecting freedom, family, and the sanctity of life.

A biblically based agenda will lead us to say what most needs to be said rather than what attracts the largest audience. It is ESA's commitment to letting the Bible rather than ideology set the agenda, which leads us to what we call a consistent pro-life stance. A consistent pro-life approach means a concern for both freedom and peace, economic justice and the family. It leads us to oppose both abortion and the arms race. Now that is not always easy. In fact, it is often tough administratively and in other ways. I sometimes meet folks who say, "I agree with you on five of six issues that you talked about, but I really do not buy the sixth one. Can I be a member of ESA?" I usually respond, "Sure, if you want to identify with a national movement that has this set of concerns, and if you are willing to say you agree on these five and want to keep listening and learning about why we take the stand we do on the sixth, then come along. Let's continue the dialogue. If after a time you find out that is really not the way you want to go, then it will be all right for you to find another organizational home for your concern for public life."

But building that biblically based agenda is not easy. My hope is that we can maintain that consistent pro-life agenda, because I believe it is biblical even though it is not a widely popular stand just now.

But that may change. I see the outlines of a new coalition that could take shape. Notice the way Catholic bishops have been speaking out for economic justice, nuclear disarmament, and the sacredness of human life. It is interesting how some of the mainline churches have begun to reconsider their stand on abortion. It is wonderful to have some of the Pro-lifers for Survival here with us this weekend.

A new political coalition could emerge that is pro-family, pro-economic justice, pro-disarmament, pro-life. It is hard to know. We can't predict the future. But whatever the political future brings, we will remain faithful to the biblical agenda whether that means going to jail or going to the White House.

Love and truth in debate. Eighth, we need both love and truth in debate. Evangelicals around the world stand at a difficult and dangerous moment. We have come to enormous prominence and visibility in society. But there is also fantastic disagreement on all kinds of issues. It would be quite easy for the evangelical movement to self-destruct in the next decade over those differences. We are being used by political movements on the left and on the right. It is a nasty time of harsh attack, distortion, dishonesty. I am afraid it will get worse before it gets better. What do we do about that? Six things, I think, will be helpful.

First of all, we need to accept the fact that Christians rightly disagree over significant issues. Honest Christians equally committed to the Scriptures can disagree. When we move from biblical principles to very specific, concrete public policies, all kinds of factors go into that decision. Even when you are doing your best to be biblical and doing your best to get the facts straight, it is still very possible to disagree. We need to accept that.

I debated with a brother who has said that it is quite possible that we will have a nuclear war that will destroy civilization. He also said that perhaps biblical Christians have come to influence just at this point in history because, since we believe in life after death, we will be willing to risk destroying the world to preserve freedom! I think that is a very, very wrong position. But that guy is my brother. I respect him at many levels. We need to accept the fact that Christians disagree. It doesn't make everything relative. It doesn't mean one idea is as good as another. But it does mean we continue trying to understand and love one another.

A second thing we need to do is get our facts straight. It is very important that we know what we are talking about. To do that, we need to talk with all kinds of people. ESA has astonished folk in Washington as our executive director and others on the staff have gone all over the place to put together Intercessors for Peace and Freedom in a way that gets the facts straight. We have gone to the right to get instances of violations of liberty, and we have checked those alleged stories out with people from another perspective. We have done the same in reverse. We have astonished people. That, apparently, is not normal procedure. We cannot afford to get our facts wrong, to exaggerate, or to distort.

Third, when we are attacked (and I speak as someone who has had a bit of experience in that area!), it is crucial that we listen openly to the criticism to see what we can learn. Most people, no matter how wrongheaded, probably have a point at some level. But then, it is crucial, also, to carry on with the biblical agenda that we believe God has given us and not worry too much about the attack. John Montgomery, whom some of you know, is a very dear friend of mine. He was a major professor of mine for two years. He helped to stabilize my faith at a time of great intellectual doubt. I was talking with John about personal attacks and criticism earlier this year over a wonderful dinner together in Philadelphia. As I was sharing some of the struggle, he laughed and said, "You know what I do? I just stay one book ahead of them. They keep firing away, but I am on to the next thing, and I do not worry about it." We need to listen hard to see what God may be saying to us when we are attacked. But then we must stick to our biblical agenda and not be worried.

Fourth, we need to avoid stereotypes and name-calling. Now, I think it is safe to say that President Reagan and I disagree about some things. It is also safe to say that I disagree vigorously with his nuclear policy. But I think it would be very wrong of me to say that President Reagan is a warmonger. I believe that the president wants peace just as much as I do. I believe very deeply that the policy he is following is likely to lead to war, and it is okay and right for me to say that. But it would be wrong of me to say that he is a warmonger, just as it would be wrong for him or someone else to say—because I think that a nuclear freeze is a good way to preserve peace, and somebody else thinks that is dangerous—that I am a Marxist. Again, we need to avoid stereotypes and name-calling.

Fifth, it would be very valuable if we could resolve to listen so hard to a person with whom we disagree that we can state that other person's position in such a way that the other person says, "Yes, that is what I mean. Now if you disagree with that, then we have an argument." There is a sense in which we do not have a right publicly to attack another person's position until we have listened that carefully to what they are saying. I understand that is a high standard and that I have not always managed, but I would like to strive for it in the future.

And finally, we need to keep seeking dialogue—dialogue in which we explain to one another on biblical grounds why we are taking certain public stands. Richard Mouw has said that it would be a fantastic thing if people like Senator Helms and Senator Hatfield would sit down about every three weeks and explain to each other, on the basis of the Bible, why they voted the way they did in the preceding three weeks. Now, you probably have your own private guess and so do I about who would change more. But that is not really important at the moment. The important thing is that they would begin to go back to the Scriptures together and let God's Word be the norm for their debate. Now, I think that same point can be applied at every level. There are folks in your local community that disagree with what your ESA local chapter is doing. You could find ways to engage in precisely that kind of dialogue. I have tried to do that in some modest ways. In the past year I have met with some of my sharpest critics—Franky Schaeffer and the leaders at L'Abri. That is not easy. There is often no instant solution. But I believe it is crucial and important. We need love and we need truth in debate.

The future does not look easy. We may be in for some very difficult years. But I am not discouraged. If we can stay biblical at every point, we will survive and we will grow stronger, even in the worst of times. God may even use us at some future point in God's divine timing to change American history so there is a little more peace, a little more freedom, a little more justice, and a little more joy in our wonderful world. May God help us all. Amen.

CHAPTER 5

A Plea for More Radical
Conservatives and More
Conserving Radicals

On November 7–8, 1985, the Billy Graham Center at
Wheaton College and the Center on Religion and
Society (directed by Richard John Neuhaus) at the
Rockford Institute held a conference on "Bible,
Politics, and Society." Prominent evangelicals engaged
in politics (e.g., Jerry Falwell's vice president, Edward
Dobson; Tim LaHaye; Richard Mouw; Richard John
Neuhaus; James Skillen) were present. I gave a paper
(a slightly different version of my lecture at Harvard
on May 16, 1983, printed in chapter 3). I was dis-
mayed to hear how some conservatives felt that the
critique of their views by people like me felt exceedingly harsh, loud, unfair, and disrespectful. ("Urinated
upon" was how one person expressed it.) My notes
from the conference indicate that I felt moved to try to
write an article that would open doors to better dialogue with people who disagreed strongly with my
political views. Just a couple days later, on a long flight
to Hong Kong, the basic ideas for this piece took
shape. *The Christian Century* printed a version of this
piece in its October 1, 1986, issue. I proposed the
attached "Covenant of Evangelical Integrity" at the

meeting of the Evangelical Roundtable at Eastern College, June 4–6, 1986.

Many of the specifics cited here (e.g., the dictatorships in South Korea and the Philippines) have changed. But the huge division in the Christian, especially the evangelical, world over Donald Trump demonstrates that the problems discussed here are even vastly greater today than in 1983. Tragically, the kind of honest dialogue called for here never happened.

One of the ironies of our time is that just as evangelical Christianity approaches a time of maximum potential impact on American public life, it threatens to self-destruct in a blaze of ferocious fratricide!

Never in this century has the opportunity for evangelical influence been greater. From conservative fundamentalists to radical evangelicals, involvement in public life is now a mandate rather than a sin. From *Sojourners* magazine to Evangelicals for Social Action to *Christianity Today*'s Institute to Pat Robertson's School of Public Policy to Jerry Falwell's Moral Majority (now Liberty Federation), theologically conservative Christians have entered the political arena with a new intensity, sophistication, and acceptance.

But the agreement ends with the consensus that evangelicals must be involved. Jerry Falwell and I—both evangelical Christians—disagree enormously over the specific direction that biblical faithfulness demands for public life.

Nor is it surprising that the vast differences increasingly spawn vicious name-calling and distorted attacks. If unchecked, they will quickly destroy our historic opportunity.

What can be done?

Three things would help: (1) a greater willingness to listen to and affirm the strong points in the critiques presented by one's "opponents"; (2) greater self-awareness about the complex elements that contribute to political judgments and an honest search for the precise location of the areas of disagreement; and (3) a new covenant of respect, integrity, and biblical faithfulness in debate.

First a word on definitions. I take the essence of a conservative attitude to be a tendency to treasure the way things are and have been in the belief that what has survived the test of time is more likely to be valuable than new untested ideas. I take the heart of a radical approach to be a tendency to challenge fundamentally the way things are and have been because of a passionate commitment to an as yet unimplemented vision of what should be.

Acknowledging Each Other's Strengths

It is striking that the conservative attack on radical evangelicals often has a somewhat similar parallel to the radical attack on conservative evangelicals.

Conservatives denounce radicals for overemphasizing economic justice and neglecting religious and political freedom. Radicals charge that conservatives neglect justice and exaggerate the importance of freedom.

Furthermore, both accuse each other of bad faith. Each charges that the other's alleged one-sidedness is really an ideological cover for even more dreadful errors. Conservatives, radicals suggest, stress democratic process and freedom more than justice in order to rationalize the self-interest of economic forces that exploit the poor. In their more hostile moments, radicals even question the motives of neoconservatives as they note the huge sums of conservative money flowing into obliging neoconservative think tanks and movements. Conservatives fear that the radicals' alleged preference for justice over freedom conceals Marxist sympathies or at least a culpable naivete about the evils of communist totalitarianism.

Both charge each other with ideological blindness. Conservatives, radicals charge, are blind to the evils produced by the American system. In their defense of "democratic capitalism," they ignore the many documented instances of unjust actions by American multi-national corporations in Latin America and elsewhere. The weak excuses offered for American cooperation with dictators in places like Chile, the Philippines, South Korea merely illustrates the blinding effect of right-wing ideology. Conservatives, on the other hand, charge radicals with a stubborn unwillingness to acknowledge the evils of totalitarian Marxism. Radicals, they claim, selectively criticize Western-oriented dictators and seldom denounce the flagrant abuse of human rights in communist countries. And when radicals describe the Sandinistas' murder of Miskito Indians in Nicaragua as "mistakes" allegedly caused by US foreign policy, they simply reveal the depth of their left-wing prejudice.

Quite naturally, both accuse each other of distorting the facts. For instance, radicals charge that conservatives dishonestly accept President Reagan's line that El Salvador's election was a democratic success and Nicaragua's a totalitarian fraud, even though independent observers indicate that the Nicaraguan election was at least as honest and fair as the one in El Salvador. Radicals, conservatives charge, ignore the evidence of a strong Marxist-Leninist element in the Sandinista Party and their growing list of human rights violations.

It is hardly surprising that these parallel charges of one-sided concerns, ideological blindness, and distorted facts lead to harsh language. Radicals are compared with Stalin and are labeled Marxist or at least naive fellow travelers. (I can cite many examples of this.) And conservatives are compared with Hitler and called fascists or at least callous oppressors without an ounce of compassion. (I don't know any examples of this, but I do know conservatives feel they are so labeled.) "I feel urinated on," one conservative leader angrily protested. Given the decibel level of recent accusations, the feeling is undoubtedly mutual.

I am not so naive as to suppose that disagreements of this magnitude can be solved easily or quickly. But I do believe we could make some progress if we were all willing to listen to each other a little more carefully. I think that both sides are making some good points. Everybody would profit if we could acknowledge each other's strengths.

I want to plead for conserving radicals who gladly affirm the conservatives' desire to preserve what is good in the past. Radicals should praise what is good and beautiful in America, champion the American tradition of democratic process and religious and political liberty and refuse to allow their valid critique of Western colonialism and current US policy to blind them to the evils of Marxism.

Why do some radicals hesitate to affirm the American tradition that has said to the world, "Give me your tired, your poor, your huddled masses yearning to breathe free"?[1] Why should radicals not give Memorial Day speeches praising America for her long tradition of fairly successful democratic process, which has somewhat decentralized power in a way that has allowed democracy to survive for a period of time seldom achieved in human history?

Radicals should also champion political and religious freedom as vigorously as they do economic justice. Neoconservatives have a point. Some social activists in the last couple of decades have not spoken as loudly or persistently about freedom as they have about justice. Radicals should protest when Nicaragua restricts political and religious liberty and commits human rights violations.[2]

Nor dare radicals allow their extremely important condemnation of past and present injustices committed by Western powers to dull their sensitivity to the ghastly history of Marxist-Leninist totalitarianism in this century. Marxist-Leninists have murdered millions of people in the USSR, China, Cambodia, and elsewhere. They do claim to want to conquer the world and impose an atheistic worldview and a one-party state by armed might. It is stubborn stupidity to ignore these facts. Selective criticism will not do. Denouncing the human rights violations in South Korea, Chile, and the Philippines (under Marcos) and ignoring them in Vietnam, Cuba, and Afghanistan has no integrity. Nor dare radicals overlook the fact that Marxist-Leninists are present in and try to exploit third-world movements for justice. It was important that the *Sojourners*-sponsored Peace Pentecost in May 1985 protested the Soviet invasion of Afghanistan. That kind of activity should be a regular item on the radical agenda.

One sign that radicals are biblically faithful rather than ideologically captive will be their readiness to champion religious and political liberty as vigorously as justice and peace.

At the same time, I want to plead for radical conservatives who are ready to critique and abandon what was not good in the past. Radical conservatives should more frequently criticize the evils of US policy at home and abroad, defend economic justice as vigorously as liberty, and refuse to allow their valid opposition to Marxism-Leninism to lead them to misperceive all third-world movements for social change as Marxist-Leninist fronts.

Why do conservatives not admit more often the frightening way that power is concentrated in the US? The enormous economic power of the very large corporations that also own the media and influence the church and the universities provides enormous political clout. Consequently, our democratic process is not nearly as free and genuine as is often claimed.

A great deal is very wrong in US policy toward the third-world. Michael Novak is surely correct when he argues that the US is not the cause of most poverty in Latin America. But he is just as surely wrong when he fails to denounce the way US multinationals and the CIA have contributed to tragedy and injustice in places like Guatemala, Chile, and Nicaragua. I would agree that on balance the Soviet Union contributes to more evil in the world than does the US. But that is no reason for dishonestly neglecting to denounce the evils of Western capitalism. When one adds up the millions murdered by the communists, one also needs to count up Native Americans, Black slaves, third-world children, and others who have died by the millions because of Western policies. In the Bible, the prophets denounced their own society's evils more often than they condemned national enemies. If conservatives would be more forthright and balanced in their condemnation of American evils, radicals might become more vigorous in their praise of the good.

Furthermore, should not economic justice be as important a concern as liberty for conservatives? Why doesn't the prophets' ringing call for justice for the poor pulse more vigorously through conservative writings? Should not conservatives acknowledge the Sandinistas' improvements in economic justice (e.g., the greater availability of education and health care to the poor) at the same time that they denounce their abuses of human rights? Should not conservatives lead the denunciation of economic injustice in places like South Korea and Central America?

Nor dare conservatives permit their important critique of Marxism-Leninism to exaggerate the presence of Marxist-Leninists in liberation movements in the third world. The first thing that needs to be said about Marcos's Philippines, Central America, or South Africa is that gross injustice cries out for prompt correction. When massive poverty, widespread starvation, and malnutrition exist alongside the concentration of land in the hands of small elites who grow export crops for wealthy nations rather than subsistence crops for their suffering neighbors, you do not need Marxist-Leninists to tell you something is wrong. Vigorous movements demanding economic justice naturally arise. To be sure, Marxist-Leninists are there to exploit this valid desire for change. (There are also democratic socialists and non-atheistic Christian Marxists who dare not be equated with Marxist-Leninists.) And since the Marxist-Leninists are ruthless and well organized, we who care about freedom as well as justice dare not be blind to their totalitarian goals. But to defend South Africa's President Botha and the Philippines' President Marcos as Jerry Falwell has done in order to protect freedom "from a possible Marxist takeover" is merely to play into the hands of the communists. Western defense of injustice makes Marxism-Leninism appear as the only hope for genuine social change. Precisely because they want to prevent more Marxist-Leninist governments in the world, conservatives should lead the attack on economic injustice around the world.

Nor is selective criticism acceptable. Why don't the Institute on Religion and Democracy and the National Association of Evangelicals condemn human rights violations in El Salvador, Guatemala, and the Philippines as vigorously and frequently as they condemn human rights violations in Nicaragua? Should not the same standards apply in all places? One sign that conservatives care more about biblical revelation than right-wing ideology will be when their words and actions demonstrate that economic justice and peace are as important to them as freedom and democracy.

More Attention to the Precise Areas of Disagreement over Political Judgments

Reaching a conclusion about the best or most biblically faithful domestic policy on welfare or foreign policy toward South Africa is an exceedingly complex undertaking. It demands more than a few biblical proof texts and a casual glance at the morning paper. I think evangelicals would understand their different political conclusions better and progress more quickly toward resolving their disagreements if they were more self-conscious about all the components that contribute to their political decisions and tried harder to isolate the precise areas of disagreement.

There are at least four crucial components in any political judgment by Christians: (1) each person's personal history and ideological background; (2) one's interpretation of the Bible; (3) one's reading of history; and (4) carefully examined generalizations (some would call such a set of generalizations an ideology) that are consciously derived from the above, especially 2 and 3.

We all bring along assumptions and convictions from our family, church, and education. Mine include the individualism and free enterprise assumptions of a typical farm boy; the biblical assumptions derived from devout, pietistic, Anabaptist parents and church; and the influence of both socialist and antisocialist professors in college. Anyone who wants to be biblical must vigorously and consciously seek to evaluate every element of inherited ideology on the basis of the Scriptures. But no one should pretend to have succeeded fully. Therefore, we should always welcome others who help us discover ways that unconsciously inherited ideology—whether of the left or right—still shapes our thinking.

The Bible is the crucial norm for all political judgments of those who want a biblically informed political agenda. But a common commitment to biblical authority does not preclude major disagreement.

Sometimes we disagree over the exegesis of specific texts. For instance, I am inclined to think that although the literal meaning of Matthew 25 is that Christians must feed and clothe brothers and sisters in Christ, nevertheless, Jesus' extension of neighbor love to include everyone in need (Matthew 5:43-44) means that Matthew 25 also summons Christians to offer food and clothing to all the needy they can assist. Others limit the application of Matthew 25 to fellow Christians. The way to overcome disagreements on specific exegesis is to do our exegesis more carefully and do it together with those who challenge our interpretations.

Sometimes we disagree when we attempt to summarize the central themes of the Scriptures or when we try to state a comprehensive overview of the biblical teaching on a particular area such as the family or economic justice. When I try to listen carefully and systematically to what the Bible says about economic justice, I hear the Bible saying that God has a special concern for the poor, weak, and marginalized; that God is opposed to extremes of wealth and poverty; and that God, as the only absolute owner, wants the productive resources of the earth distributed in a decentralized way so that individuals and families can earn their own way and cooperate with God in the shaping of history. (Therefore, I am not a socialist, if socialism means state ownership of the means of production. I believe decentralized, limited private ownership, rather than the concentration of power as in state ownership or huge corporations, is what the Bible suggests.) Others disagree vigorously. Again, the way to make progress on these disagreements is to challenge the specific biblical work that provides the foundation for each other's biblical generalizations.

Sometimes we disagree over more fundamental hermeneutical questions. Anabaptists, dispensationalists, and Reformed thinkers all bring different assumptions about the relationship between the Old and New Testaments to their understanding of the text. Those assumptions as well as others obviously affect how each of us relates the biblical material to specific public policy proposals for contemporary secular societies. Hermeneutical differences are harder to resolve. Nevertheless, we should try to help each other see where we think a more faithful reading of all Scripture would lead to different hermeneutical assumptions.

Our different readings of history are a third area of disagreement. We often differ both in our interpretation of the broad sweep of history and in our understanding of what is really the case (the "facts") in a particular situation. My reading of history leads me to conclude that the history of twentieth-century Marxist-Leninist states shows that in spite of some positive results, their overall impact has been so negative that we ought to vigorously resist any expansion of Marxism-Leninism. Another broad historical assumption of mine is that Western colonialism has had massive evil components as well as positive elements. Others would disagree vigorously.

Similarly, it is not easy to agree even on specific "facts." What "really happened" when the pope visited Managua? How strong is the hardcore Marxist-Leninist element in the Sandinista Party? If my answer to the latter question had been "totally dominant," I would have supported a different US policy toward Nicaragua than I have in the last seven years.

Disagreements over matters of fact are difficult but not impossible to resolve. If they result from a mere lack of information, sharing facts will help. Joint exploration by groups like Evangelicals for Social Action and the Institute for Religion and Democracy is one way to resolve different interpretations of the facts in places like Nicaragua or South Korea. If either side is afraid of such a joint exploration, the public ought to know and draw the appropriate conclusions. If disagreements result from conflicting methodologies in the social sciences, the process of adjudication is far more complex but not impossible. We dare not give up the attempt to help each other see the facts more accurately. Whether the impact of British colonialism in Nigeria or US political and economic involvement in the Philippines has been positive is a factual question. If we refuse to confuse such disagreements with moral failure and instead look more carefully at the data together, we will make more progress.

Finally, we disagree over the broad generalizations (or ideology) that we consciously derive from the complex of previous decisions. I believe that on balance a market economy (with certain parameters to restrict injustice) rather than a state-owned, centrally planned economy as in the USSR is more likely to produce both freedom and justice. I believe that a pluralistic political process with more than one political party is more likely to produce liberty. And I believe that many independent centers of power (church, media, economic life, education, the state) rather than one center of state power controlling all the others leads more surely to peace, justice, and freedom. Again, others—including faithful Christians—disagree.

If we can become clear about precisely where we disagree, we can at least understand each other better. And we can probably proceed more quickly to lessening the disagreements. It is essential that a disagreement over the specific exegesis of Matthew 25 not be misconstrued as an immoral lack of compassion for the poor or Marxist-Leninist politics. If you disagree with people here, you need to question their exegesis, not their compassion or their politics. It is tragically misleading to see a different judgment about the degree of Marxist-Leninist influence in the Sandinista Party as an ideological commitment to Marxism-Leninism. If you disagree, you need to challenge their facts, not their commitment to democracy. It is dishonest to portray an honest conclusion from history and the Bible that democratic capitalism is the surest path to justice for the poor as a lack of compassion. If you disagree, you need to question their broad reading of history and the Scriptures, not their concern for the poor. If evangelicals are to make a maximal contribution to American public life, they must pay much more careful attention to the precise areas of disagreement.

A New Covenant of Integrity in Debate

Finally, we need a new covenant to dialogue civilly, honestly, fairly, and biblically. The debate should flow fast but not furious, vigorous but not vicious. In particular, the evangelical leadership needs to enter into a mutual covenant personally to avoid and publicly to condemn name-calling and slanderous stereotyping; inaccurate, one-sided depictions of others' positions; distortion of the facts; and unwillingness to test one's views with others' views on the basis of the Scriptures.

The level of name-calling and malicious stereotyping has ballooned in the last few years. I disagree intensely with President Reagan's nuclear policy. But I believe he desires peace in the world as much as I do. It is valid for me to argue that his nuclear buildup will probably lead to nuclear war, but it is immoral name-calling to call him a warmonger. Similarly, it is quite proper for someone to charge that my advocacy of a bilateral, verifiable nuclear freeze increases the danger of nuclear war or even a Soviet takeover, but it is slander to call me a Marxist.

There is also a difference between honest categorizing and malicious stereotyping. We cannot avoid using categories for people and movements. It is not wrong to think that on nuclear policy, I tend toward a liberal-left stance and Jerry Falwell toward a conservative-right position. But it would be very wrong to ignore Falwell's repeated affirmation of democratic pluralism and separation of church and state and imply that he is a fascist. Similarly, it would be dishonest to ignore my repeated repudiation of Marxism-Leninism and marshal selective quotations to imply that I secretly favor Marxist-Leninist totalitarianism.

We need a new covenant to portray each other's opinions fairly. We all know how tempting it is to exaggerate one aspect and ignore another side of an opponent's perspective. There is a fairly simple way to check whether we have accurately understood and fairly summarized another's views. We can ask the other person! I suspect that at least half of the current battles in church circles would end if the major contestants merely consulted each other personally and directly to see if the views they were denouncing were actually held by the other person. One criterion of honesty in debate is that we state the views of a person we criticize in such a way that that person says, "Yes, that is what I mean."

Until we do that, we have no right to criticize. Of course, people may sometimes dishonestly deny what they are actually saying. There must be room for showing carefully and factually that persons pretend to be something other than what they really are. Nor am I saying we can never object to another person's views without picking up the telephone. But I think we would make an enormous step forward if the evangelical leadership would covenant together not to engage in any major public criticism of each other until they had personally checked with the other party to make sure they were accurately stating the other's views.

We must also get our facts straight. We dare not continue to accept a situation where different Christian organizations offer the public contradictory facts and then refuse to meet together or search together to resolve the contradictions. The most rigorous submission to the facts, however unpleasant, is essential for maximal evangelical impact on public life.

Finally, we need a new covenant to search the Scriptures together. It is a farce to have Jerry Falwell and me continue forever telling the American public that our mutually contradictory public policy stands are thoroughly biblical. There is a way to work at that. Evangelical leaders could sit down privately twice a year for two days of confidential conversation and explain prayerfully and openly to each other the biblical foundations of our different political proposals. As we survey church history, we see that even Augustine, Luther, Calvin, and Wesley occasionally got it wrong. We ought to conclude that since we are making at least as many mistakes, we desperately need the insight of other Christian leaders who are striving to submit their total lives to biblical revelation. (I know that some try very hard to do this and that others persistently refuse to cooperate.) One criterion of the integrity of evangelical political leadership should be a willingness to regularly test the biblical validity of one's views with other biblically committed Christian leaders.

In the late twentieth century, evangelicals face an unprecedented opportunity. In order not to squander it, we need a new openness to acknowledge the valid arguments of those who disagree with us, greater self-awareness of the precise areas of our disagreement, and a new covenant of integrity in debate. Even if all that happened by special supernatural intervention, we would still have different perspectives and organizations. But radicals would adopt some conservative strengths, and conservatives would affirm some radical solutions.

Is it too much to ask God to give us more conserving radicals and more radical conservatives?

A Covenant of Evangelical Integrity

Evangelicals today enjoy a historic opportunity of increased impact on church and society. At the same time, sharp internal division threatens enervating weakness and even self-destruction.

We, the undersigned evangelical leaders, therefore, renewing our confession of the orthodox truths of historic Christianity and submitting our total thought and action unconditionally to Jesus Christ and the Scriptures of the Old and New Testament, covenant together to debate our ongoing differences civilly, honestly and biblically.

In particular, we covenant that as God gives us grace, we will seek to avoid name-calling and misrepresentation of one another's views and to practice mutual submission by regularly testing our understanding of the Bible and the world with that of evangelical leaders who disagree with us.

To avoid name-calling, we covenant together to seek to observe the difference between honest categorizing and malicious stereotyping.

To avoid misrepresenting one another's views, we covenant that we will, before publicly criticizing other brothers or sisters, seek to

88

state their views in such a way that they will see we have honestly tried to reflect their viewpoint accurately. When in doubt, we will directly contact other leaders to make sure we are not misrepresenting them.

To promote honest submission to the facts, we covenant to engage in joint exploration of disputed data as time and finances permit.

To promote continual reformation of our thinking in submission to the Scriptures, we covenant to, once a year, if at all possible, engage in two days of confidential discussion, listening to and dialoguing with other evangelical leaders who wish to challenge us on the basis of God's revealed Word.

Note
1. Emma Lazarus, "The New Colossus," https://www.poetryfoundation.org/poems/46550/the-new-colossus.
2. As Jim Wallis does in *Sojourners*, January 1986, 4–5.

CHAPTER 6

God's Invitation to Shalom

I initially presented this message on November 21, 1985, at an American Baptist Peace Conference at the First Baptist Church of St. Paul, Minnesota. I gave versions of the speech at least three dozen times in many places in North America, Australia, India, Sweden, England, New Zealand, and (Communist) East Germany.

In the thirty-five years since I first gave this speech, the world has made quite amazing progress in substantially reducing the percentage of people living in poverty—progress which I describe in the later editions of my book *Rich Christians in an Age of Hunger* (see the sixth edition, 2015).

My belief that the church should greatly expand its use of nonviolent techniques has grown stronger over the years, as shown in my book *Nonviolent Action: What Christian Ethics Demands but Most Christians Have Never Really Tried* (2015).

Over the years, I have also made it clearer that defining Jesus' gospel as the Good News of the kingdom is absolutely crucial (see my *Good News and Good Works,* 1999). One of the primary reasons for the dreadful moral failure of so many in the Christian church (especially evangelicals) is that they have reduced the gospel to the idea that Jesus came to die on the cross so that our sins could be forgiven and we could go to heaven when we die. When people limit their understanding of the gospel to that partial truth, they fundamentally undermine the importance of Christian ethics and living like Jesus.

"Blessed are the peacemakers," Jesus said, "for they will be called children of God" (Matthew 5:9, NIV). You and I are called to be peacemakers in the most dangerous twenty years in human history.

Now, that is a heavy way to start a peace conference. But it is realistic. At the same time, it is important that we not lose sight of the goodness and beauty of our world. This world is a fantastic place. It is a lovely planet. That was symbolized for me in many ways: by a wonderful Lutheran retreat spot up in the upper Cascades where I have had the privilege to go and speak with my family; by the eyes and smile of my wife as I return from a ten-day trip abroad. This is a gorgeous world, a wonderful gift from the hand of the Creator. As Augustine said, it is a ring from our Beloved.

But the beauty of creation has been tragically marred. There is dreadful brokenness in our world, in our homes, in our environment. The divorce rate reminds us of the incredible pain and hell in our families. Newspaper headlines about pollution and acid rain remind us of how careless we are with our environment. The international global economy is full of brokenness. Some thirty-five thousand children have died of starvation today. One billion people live in desperate poverty. In the international political community, there is chaos and disorder. Human rights and democratic freedoms are trampled on. In many parts of the world, the arms race seems to spiral ever upward. What's wrong?

There are lots of answers to that, as you know. Freud gives us a psychological answer. Marx gives us an economic answer. And there are important truths in those answers. But the Bible, I believe, takes us much deeper. The Bible says you and I are made for right relationship with the Creator, our neighbor, and the earth. And the Bible says that if we mess up our relationship with

God, then we introduce terrible disorder and chaos with neighbor and the earth.

We are made for living in shalom with God and neighbor, and our hearts and societies are restless, indeed tormented, until they rest in that divine shalom.

Notice that I am using the word *shalom*. That is the Hebrew word for peace. It is a much richer word than our English word *peace*. It means far more than simply the absence of fighting. It means material well-being, a land flowing with milk and honey. It means justice. It means right relationship with neighbor so that everyone has the means to earn their own way. The psalmist says that "righteousness and peace kiss each other" (Psalm 85:10, NIV), and Isaiah says that the effect of justice will be shalom. It means right relationship in the family. It means inner peace, that kind of inner peace and security that come from knowing that God is like a mother eagle who pushes us out of the nest to teach us to fly and then gently catches us as we fall. Certainly, it means the absence of war. And above all it means right relationship with God.

The whole story of salvation is an unending invitation from God to shalom. The fall messed up human relationships in an incredible way. When we rebelled proudly and stupidly against God, we introduced hell into human affairs. But God did not give up. God called a special people, the people of Israel. God told them how God wanted them to live in right relationship with God and with neighbor. God said, "Worship only me." And God said, "Deal justly with everyone in your society, share the land; make sure that the poor are not oppressed." But Israel constantly broke that shalom with God and neighbor. They fell into idolatry, and they were very unjust. So, God sent the prophets to warn that they must return to God's shalom or there would be trouble. But they refused. So, God said that their societies would have to be destroyed.

But even then, God refused to abandon us. Through the prophets, God promised a time when the Messiah would come to

bring shalom in a new way. The prophets looked ahead to a
future day when there would be shalom—fantastic, radically
transformed, right relationships between us and God and also
with neighbors. As Jeremiah 31:31-34 (NIV) shows, right relationship with God was central to the prophetic vision of messianic
shalom. Jeremiah said,

> "The days are coming" declares the LORD,
> "when I will make a new covenant
> with the people of Israel
> and with the people of Judah. . . .
> I will put my law in their minds
> and write it on their hearts.
> I will be their God,
> and they will be my people.
> No longer will they teach their neighbor,
> or say to one another, 'Know the LORD,'
> because they will all know me,
> from the least of them to the greatest,"
> declares the LORD.
> "For I will forgive their wickedness
> and will remember their sins no more."

Right relationship with neighbor was equally central to the messianic hope for shalom. Micah looked for the messianic time
when they would "beat their swords into plowshares and their
spears into pruning hooks. Nation will not take up sword against
nation, nor will they train for war anymore" (Micah 4:3, NIV).

And in the ringing words of Isaiah:

> For to us a child is born,
> to us a son is given,
> and the government will be on his shoulders.
> And he will be called

> Wonderful Counselor, Mighty God,
> Everlasting Father, Prince of Peace.
> Of the greatness of his government and peace
> there will be no end.
> He will reign on David's throne
> and over his kingdom,
> establishing and upholding it
> with justice and righteousness
> from that time on and forever.
> —Isaiah 9:6-7, NIV

That messianic hope, the early church proclaimed, was fulfilled in the Carpenter of Nazareth. "Peace on earth," the angels sang when the babe of Bethlehem was born. Shivers of excitement must have raced through first-century Jewish hearts when Jesus announced the welcome news: "The time has come. The kingdom of God has come near. Repent and believe the good news!" (Mark 1:15, NIV).

But what did he mean? There is increasing scholarly agreement that Jesus meant two things: He meant that he was the long-expected Messiah. And he meant that his messianic kingdom was breaking into the present.

There has been vigorous debate, of course, about whether or not Jesus thought the kingdom which he was announcing was entirely future or, as others have said, entirely present, or perhaps partly present and partly future. But there is growing agreement that in striking contrast to Jewish thought, Jesus viewed the kingdom as both present and future. The Jews looked forward to a supernatural shaking when the Messiah would come to destroy Israel's national enemies in a bloody battle. He would initiate a new age of messianic peace after that battle. In Jewish expectation, there was a radical, sharp break between the old age and the new messianic age.

Jesus, on the other hand, taught that the messianic age had truly broken into this old world. Its powers, the powers of the messianic kingdom, were already at work in our time in his person and in his work, even though the kingdom, of course, will come in its fullness only at his return.

But what was the nature of this kingdom that Jesus announced? Was it a political order like that of Rome? Or was it an invisible spirituality in the hearts of isolated individuals? Neither of those things. Rather, it was shalom, the right relationships with God and neighbor that come when one accepts Jesus' messianic proclamation of God's reign breaking in. It is as Matthew 6:33 says, the shalom that comes when we seek first the new kingdom and its righteousness (its right relationships). And as the Lord's Prayer makes clear, it is the visible social order of Jesus' new disciples that comes when God's will is done on earth as it is in heaven (Matthew 6:10).

God's peace, God's shalom, is a divine gift. If anything is clear in Jesus, it is that we enter this new messianic kingdom by sheer grace and forgiveness, not by human effort and merit, and certainly not by mere societal engineering. Jesus disagreed sharply with the Pharisees. Many Pharisees thought that the coming of the messianic kingdom would be hastened if all the Jews would obey the law. Jesus, on the other hand, insisted that one enters the kingdom by sheer grace, as a little child. "For the kingdom of heaven is like a landowner who went out early in the morning to hire workers for his vineyard" (Matthew 20:1, NIV). No matter how long the laborers worked, they all received the same salary. In his parables, Jesus taught that God is a forgiving Father who seeks lost sheep (Luke 15:3-7) and forgives prodigal sons and daughters (Luke 15:11-32).

Jesus' actions matched his words. To the extreme annoyance of the self-righteous Pharisees, Jesus associated with prostitutes and tax collectors. He forgave such sinners because he knew that God in heaven is like the father of the prodigal son. It was the same understanding that led him to the cross to die as the substitute for the sins of all who would believe on him and repent. Central to the shalom of Jesus' messianic kingdom is the New Testament teaching that it is a gift, a divine gift, for sinners who repent and accept God's unconditional forgiveness through the cross. When we accept that divine grace, then truly, as Paul says in Romans 5:1, we have peace with God.

Equally important, however, to an understanding of the messianic kingdom that Jesus proclaimed is the fact that it was also a new social order—a new social order in which all things were being restored to that shalom, to that set of right relationships intended by the Creator.

God's shalom is also a task. Jesus formed a circle of disciples, and together this new messianic community began to model a challenge to the status quo at many points where it was wrong.

Jesus upset men. Men were happy with the easy divorce laws that enabled them to dismiss their wives on almost any pretext. He insisted that God intended one man and one woman to live together in lifelong covenant. Jesus also disregarded social patterns that treated women as inferior. According to the customs of the time, a woman's word had no weight whatsoever in court. It was a disgrace for men to appear publicly with women. A widely used prayer recommended for daily use by Jewish men thanked God that they had not been created a Gentile, a slave, or a woman. Jesus, on the other hand, appeared publicly with women, taught them theology, and honored them with his first resurrection appearance. Jesus upset political rulers. They were smugly satisfied with their domination of their subjects. In the dawning messianic age, servanthood must replace domination. The greatest in the kingdom is the Messiah, who is servant of all. Therefore, those who aspire to leadership in Jesus' kingdom must likewise be humble servants rather than domineering masters.

Jesus terrified the economic establishment of his day. He said it would be easier for a camel to squeeze through the eye of a needle than for a rich person to enter the kingdom. He summoned those with capital to lend and make loans even if they had no hope of getting it back. He recognized the rich young ruler as a man full of that idolatrous materialism that plagues many rich people. And so he summoned him—and presumably all people who worship the same idol—to give all his wealth to the poor. And he denounced those who oppressed poor widows.

Most astonishing of all, perhaps, Jesus taught that right relationship with neighbor included love even for vicious enemies. "You have heard that it was said, 'Love your neighbor and hate your enemy.' But I tell you, love your enemies and pray for those who persecute you, that you may be children of your Father in heaven" (Matthew 5:43-45, NIV). Rejecting ethnic limitations on neighbor love, rejecting violence and retaliation, Jesus taught his circle of followers to abandon the old age's search for shalom through the sword. Imitating the perfection of the Father in heaven means loving one's enemies.

It is crucial to see that the new messianic kingdom Jesus announced involved a very concrete set of right relationships between husband and wife, between men and women, between rich and poor, between oppressor and oppressed. Nor was Jesus merely talking about a private ethic for personal relations. Jesus came, after all, as the Messiah of the entire Jewish people. Rich and poor, leaders and "unimportant people" listened to him. The Sermon on the Mount is Jesus' messianic manifesto to which he called the entire Jewish people.

Jesus and his disciples began to model the gospel they preached. In the circle of Jesus' disciples, there emerged a new community, a new social order. This new social order began to live out the shalom of the new reign Jesus announced. Most of Jesus' contemporaries, of course, found it hard, very hard, to believe that this carpenter's small circle of forgiven tax collectors, prostitutes, and fishermen was truly the beginning of the glorious messianic kingdom promised by the prophets. One can almost understand. Jesus' circle was too weak and too insignificant; his teaching was too demanding and costly; his claims were too presumptuous, if not indeed blasphemous. To prove he was wrong, some of the religious and political leaders had Jesus crucified.

But then, on the third day, Jesus rose from the dead. The resurrection proved to the discouraged disciples that Jesus was truly the Messiah, that Jesus' messianic kingdom had really begun. And Pentecost confirmed it. As we read Peter's sermon in Acts 2, we see clearly that it was the raising of the Crucified One and the pouring out of the Holy Spirit that convinced the early church that the messianic age predicted long ago by the prophets had truly broken into their history.

In the power of the Holy Spirit, those new Christians were truly and visibly a new community of shalom. The worst racial hostility in the ancient world—that between Jew and Gentile—dissolved as Jew and Gentile accepted each other in Jesus' new community. Slaves and women became persons. The rich shared so generously that there were no poor among them, Acts says. We are told that even in the second century, Christians were fasting three days a week to buy folk out of slavery who had accepted Christ. And they loved their enemies even while being tossed to the lions and burned at the stake. For three centuries, their teachers called on them to reject the violence of both abortion and war.

It is not surprising that this community of forgiven and transformed sinners referred to their message of salvation as the "gospel of peace." That phrase appears a number of times in Acts and the Epistles. In their own lives, they were experiencing restored relationships, shalom, with both God and neighbor. To be sure, this new community was not perfect. It had problems, but they had truly been transformed. They had, as the book of Hebrews puts it, tasted the powers of the age to come.

The present reality of the already dawning messianic kingdom anchored the early Christians' breathtaking claim and hope of cosmic restoration, cosmic shalom. They dared to believe that the crucified and risen carpenter was the key to all of human history. They dared to believe that he was now King of kings and Lord of lords. They dared to believe that at his return he would complete his victory over every ruler and authority, even death itself, and bring all things into subjection to God. They even believed that creation itself would be freed from its bondage and decay and experience the glorious freedom and wholeness of the children of God. Even though they were an almost infinitesimally insignificant minority in a powerful pagan empire, they dared to proclaim that God would reconcile all things in heaven and on earth through the cross of this humble carpenter. They dared to hope for that cosmic completion of the shalom Jesus announced precisely because the resurrection and Pentecost were solid, tangible evidence that the messianic reign had truly begun.

Since we Christians know where history is going, since we know the kingdom of shalom will surely come, you and I have the courage and strength to work now to establish signs of that coming shalom in our personal lives, in our families, in our churches, and in our societies.

We saw that in the Scriptures, shalom starts with a right relationship with God. So that is where Christian peacemakers will also start to build shalom. Let us never accept the naive notion of the Enlightenment and Marxism that we can create new persons by mere education, mere societal engineering, or mere structural changes in the economy. All of those are important, but alas, they do not create new persons. The human dilemma is deeper than that. It lies at the center of the ornery, selfish personalities that we are. It lies at the very core of our beings. Only transforming grace mediated by a personal relationship with God in Christ can correct that deep problem.

Biblical peacemakers, then, will emphasize evangelism. They will emphasize that people need to come into a living personal relationship with God to be changed.

We need more evangelism if there is to be more shalom in our troubled world. Jim Wallis of Sojourners believes that he is being called to hold peace revivals. That is an important, very significant development. Pray for Jim as he works on that. I wish that peace and justice activists and evangelists could reverse roles in the next decade. If some prominent evangelists would become activist crusaders for peace and justice, if some prominent social activists would become leaders in evangelism, we would see dramatic changes in the church and in the world.

There is another aspect of peace with God that is very important for us peace and justice activists. You know, it is easy for us to get so involved in our important crusades, so enmeshed in our significant techniques, statistics, and strategies that we lose the vitality of our personal relationship with Christ. Richard Lovelace, professor of church history at Gordon-Conwell Theological Seminary, has said that most of those who are praying are not praying for peace and justice. And most of those who are working for peace and justice are not praying. Now, that is not entirely true, thank God. But there is too much truth in it to leave us comfortable. That should not be. Peace and justice activists need prayer, personal devotions, and the divine intimacy of daily communion with the Divine Lover. They need that to survive, to have strength and courage.

Revelation 3:15-17 is very important for social activists: "I know your deeds, that you are neither cold nor hot. I wish you were either one or the other! So, because you are lukewarm—neither cold nor hot—I am about to spit you out of my mouth. You say, 'I am rich, I have acquired wealth and do not need a thing

(NIV).'" This word was directed to the church in the city of Laodicea. This city was a very wealthy city, very proud of its technology. It had apparently developed a very special kind of medicine that was successful in curing some eye disease, and it also had a very fine, rich white linen that was sold throughout the empire. The church there said they were rich, prosperous, in need of nothing. But what did God say from Revelations 3:17-22?

> But you do not realize that you are wretched, pitiful, poor, blind and naked. I counsel you to buy from me gold refined in the fire, so you can become rich; and white clothes to wear, so you can cover your shameful nakedness; and salve to put on your eyes, so you can see.
>
> Those whom I love I rebuke and discipline. So be earnest and repent. Here I am! I stand at the door and knock. If anyone hears my voice and opens the door, I will come in and eat with that person and they with me.

We usually apply these verses to the mainstream of our society—to materialists and their shocking way of placing material possessions above God. And that is right. That is one very important application of the text. But I think it also fits us social activists. We sometimes get so busy, so wrapped up in our techniques for social change, that we forget the inward journey. We lose the renewing awareness of the Lord in our lives. To peace and justice activists who have fallen into that satanic trap, the Lord says, "Here I am! I stand at the door and knock." Let's open our doors daily and sit down and fellowship with the risen Lord in prayer and worship and study of the Scriptures. As we do that, we will be able to return to our vital work, knowing that the battle is finally the Lord's, not ours.

A right relationship with God is the starting point for biblical peacemakers. But peace with God overflows into peace with neighbor. And that has a lot of ramifications. It includes the nearest neighbor, not just the poor peasant in India or the Soviet soldier in Afghanistan. The nearest neighbor is our spouse, our children, our parents. If I am not allowing the Holy Spirit to begin to heal the points of pain and conflict between me and my wife or between me and my children, is it not rather arrogant to suggest to the Congress that I know how to bring peace and reconciliation in the international political arena?

Our near neighbors also include the local body of believers where we worship. Your local congregation, my local congregation, is supposed to be a little picture now of what heaven is going to be like. The church should be a community of shalom. It should be far ahead of the rest of society, far ahead of our broken world. It should be modeling, living out that shalom, which God promises will come. If we are not allowing the Holy Spirit to begin to heal the sad disputes and feuds that we so often have in our local congregations, is it not strange to suggest that we know how to tell the president to resolve the complex problems in our international community? It is a farce to ask Washington to legislate what Christians refuse to live. The church has often been a missing link in our very good social action. We have rushed off to Washington without ever discovering within the local church itself a new commitment to the poor, to justice, to peacemaking.

Now, I do not mean for a minute that before we work for political change, we must have perfect marriages and perfect families. I have teenagers, so I want to be cautious. And certainly, I do not mean we have to have perfect churches. I fail, at times, at all of those points. But I believe we need to be on the way. We need to be making progress in all of those areas.

The gospel, after all, is the Good News of the messianic kingdom, that kingdom of shalom that has already begun. Therefore, whenever our churches succumb to the brokenness of the world instead of modeling God's new society, our churches are a living denial of the gospel we preach.

Biblical peacemaking, however, is not some privatized concern, restricted to our personal lives and the church. God has a cosmic plan of transformation. And so must God's people. We need to be concerned with all of life, with all of society.

Tragically, too often God's people fail to see that. A few years ago, I experienced personally one of the more astounding examples of this kind of privatized faith. I was talking to a man with very high responsibility for the testing of nuclear weapons in the United States. We had an hour together. I knew he was a very devout, committed Christian. In many ways, he was a most wonderful brother, in fact, one of the most attractive Christians I have met in a long time. So I asked him, "How do you put together what you are doing with your faith in Christ?" I thought he might say that he believed that we needed nuclear weapons even though he was horrified at the prospects (and I know, in fact, that he does think that). But that is not what he said. He said, "I believe God has called me here." He added, "I am able to evangelize folk I am working with. I am able to strengthen their families." He believed that he was called to play a key role in the testing of America's nuclear weapons because his job gave him an opportunity to evangelize!

Our faith must go beyond concerns of the family, church, and personal evangelism. If the biblical understanding of shalom controls us, then we will be very active working for peace and justice and freedom in the larger society. That means all kinds of things, and I am not going to try to spell them out tonight. It means economic justice, it means nuclear disarmament, it means human rights, freedom, democratic process. All those things are extremely important. I believe they flow from biblical faith. We are going to be talking about those things in the conference in the next couple of days, so I will not try to spell out all of that. But I want to conclude by sharing a vision for one specific new initiative that I believe the Christian church ought to consider in the next decade.

Many of you know about Witness for Peace. It is a group of American Christians who believe deeply that the US funding of the contras in Nicaragua is wrong. They are not endorsing the Sandinistas, but they believe the US action must stop. They have gone down, in groups of twenty, about three groups a month. And they go into the most dangerous areas where the contras are killing and maiming civilians every day. They try to stand with the people: to witness against that evil, to document and to report back. I have been down as a member of Witness for Peace. I did that this January. I do not claim that everything that Witness for Peace has done has been wise, but I do think it is a very important new initiative.

I wonder if the time may not be right to expand that kind of effort in a dramatic way. In the late twentieth century, global Christianity may have a unique opportunity to launch a strikingly new kind of peace initiative. What would happen if the Christian church would decide to train twenty thousand persons in what we might call an International Christian Peace Guard. The Peace Guard would be totally nonviolent. It would be sophisticated in its socioeconomic political analysis. It would be highly trained in the techniques of nonviolent direct action, developed by people like Gandhi and Martin Luther King Jr. It would be as tough as the US Marines. And it would be immersed in prayer, study of the Scriptures, and dependence on the Holy Spirit. The fundamental goal of the International Christian Peace Guard would be to promote peace and justice and democratic process in situations of conflict between nations or large societal groups within a nation. And it would work at that by placing a body of well-trained Spirit-filled Christians in the midst of warring parties.

Boulding's Law says, "If something exists, then it must be possible." (I suppose that is true!) Gandhi and Martin Luther King Jr.

demonstrated the effectiveness of nonviolent direct action. Witness for Peace has shown that nonviolent direct action can be applied to conflicts between nations and large societal groups. If this much success has been possible with only minimal preparation, only minimal training and numbers, what might a carefully planned International Christian Peace Guard accomplish?

Never has the need been greater. Standing fearfully at the end of the twentieth century, we look back horrified at the most violent one hundred years in human history. And we peer ahead anxiously to a probable future that makes past bloodshed seem as nothing. The constantly escalating cycle of violence and counterviolence demands a serious search for new paths. The growing danger of each generation of ever more deadly nuclear weapons cries out for alternatives.

General Robert Mathis is a former chief of the US Air Force. He was one of the plenary speakers at a national conference on the nuclear arms race held in Pasadena, California, in May 1983. General Mathis believes that at the present time, the Western powers must possess nuclear weapons. But I was interested in the way he responded enthusiastically to a proposal for this kind of international peace guard. Why? Precisely because he knows the devastating capability of present weapons. And therefore, he was very eager to explore significant new alternatives to war.

Both pacifist and non-pacifist Christians could join together in testing this kind of peace guard. In fact, I think the premises of both demand such an involvement. According to the just war folk, as you know, lethal violence, going to war, must always be a last resort. How can they say that resorting to war is justified until they have tested in a sophisticated, sustained way the techniques of Martin Luther King Jr. and Gandhi? Pacifists, on the other hand, hotly reject the charge that their refusal to bear arms is a callous disregard of their obligation to protect the weak neighbor from bullies and oppressors. How, then, can pacifists avoid the charge of hypocrisy unless they are ready to risk dangers comparable to those faced by soldiers in a nonviolent struggle against those who trample on the poor, the weak, and the defenseless?

The Christian community could issue a call for twenty thousand volunteers ready to give two years of their lives in costly nonviolent struggle for shalom. A carefully designed training process of four to six months would prepare highly skilled people ready to intervene nonviolently for the sake of peace and justice. The Mennonite Churches in North America are seriously considering precisely this kind of proposal.

Are the people available? Would thousands of people be ready to march into the jaws of potential suffering and death? We will not know until some courageous churches issue the call. But the history of warfare and nonviolent action strongly suggests that danger will not deter volunteers. Over human history, after all, millions of bold souls have gladly risked death for a noble cause and a grand vision.

The history of the early missionaries is instructive at this point. When war, massacre, or disease wiped out volunteers, committed replacements quickly emerged. Today's growing third-world church, now equal in size to that in the West, validates the courageous sacrifices of those pioneers, volunteers, and martyrs.

Death, of course, is not the point. To seek martyrdom would be naive and immoral. The way of Christ is the way of life, not death. But the Christian martyrs of all ages stand in silent testimony that the way to abundant life sometimes passes through the dark valley where the cross stands stark and rugged. And those who dare in loving obedience to shoulder that old rugged cross will exchange it someday for a crown of shalom in the peaceful kingdom of the reconciling Lamb. Amen.

CHAPTER 7

Rich Christians in an Age of Hunger — Revisited

I initially gave this lecture at Wheaton College on November 10, 1993, at a campus-wide public lecture sponsored by Wheaton College's Center for Applied Ethics. Professor Peter J. Hill responded.[1]

The statistics about the number and percentage of people living in poverty are outdated. As I say in my sixth (2015) edition of *Rich Christians in an Age of Hunger*, we have made quite astonishing progress in the last thirty years in reducing global poverty. Nevertheless, hundreds of millions are desperately poor and need our help today. Except for that, I still believe strongly everything else I say here.

I am often asked what I think today about my book *Rich Christians in an Age of Hunger*, which was first published in 1977.[2] Often the question occurs in an informal setting and my response is appropriately brief and unsystematic. A request to give a formal presentation on the topic, however, prompted some more extensive reflection. I see myself on a journey. I am vividly aware of both my finitude and sinful perversity. This essay represents an attempt to stop for a moment and reflect on what I have learned.

When my book *Completely Pro-Life* came out in 1987, the *Criswell Theological Review* published a fascinating review. The reviewer suggested that *Completely Pro-Life*, with its affirmation of the family and condemnation of abortion, began "the process of dehobgoblinization" of me. Perhaps this essay can continue that process.

I would like first to summarize my initial concerns in writing *Rich Christians*; second, to reflect on some of the responses (especially some of the critical ones); third, to comment on where I have changed; and finally, to point toward the future.

The first and most important reason I wrote the book was because I believed then and I believe now that Jesus is the answer to the problems of our gorgeous, twisted blue planet. Not in some simplistic way. And not the manicured, innocuous Jesus of so much American evangelicalism, but the real historical Jesus, the one who announced and demonstrated the gospel of the dawning messianic kingdom; who drove the oppressive money changers out of the temple; who went out of his way to identify with lepers, marginalized women, and poor folk; who died for our sins on the cross; and who rose bodily from the tomb on the third day. This astonishing Nazarene carpenter, true God and true man, is indeed the only Savior and only hope for our sad, broken world. But it is only as we obey Jesus' last commission in his prayer to the Father—"As you sent me into the world, I have sent them into the world" (John 17:18, NIV); only as we live what we preach, combining daring proclamation with costly servanthood, that our sharing of this glorious gospel has convincing power. If we pray as Jesus did, depend on the Spirit as Jesus did, and combine word and deed as Jesus did, then indeed we can truly expect that this real historical Jesus will use us to bring his salvation and healing to our sinful, hurting world. In short, I wrote *Rich Christians* because I long with all my heart for more and more Christians today who truly live and preach Jesus' whole gospel.

Rich Christians focused on one central area of our failure to do that, namely, our failure to live what the Bible tells us about God's concern for the poor. At the center of *Rich Christians* is the juxtaposition of three things: (1) massive global poverty and persistent widespread starvation, (2) the recurrent biblical teaching that God and God's people have a special concern for the poor, and (3) the ever-growing materialism and neglect of the poor by an expanding circle of increasingly affluent Christians living in industrialized countries.

When I wrote the first edition of *Rich Christians* in 1976, the best statistics suggested that at least one billion people lived in desperate unnecessary poverty. They had virtually no health care or education and often not enough food to develop or maintain healthy bodies. Their children's brains were often malformed for lack of protein.

When you juxtapose that data with the astonishing things the Bible says about God's concern for the poor, the impact is stunning. Lending to the poor is like lending to the Creator. Unless we seek justice for the poor, we do not know God properly. In fact, if we don't feed the hungry and clothe the naked, we will depart eternally from the living God. God and God's faithful people have a special concern for the poor.

The more carefully I examined what and how much the Bible says about the poor, the more astonished I became. My original outline for the book reserved one chapter for biblical material. But as I studied the Scriptures, that chapter grew into three and a half chapters. Those chapters, I still believe, are the best part of the book.

Incredibly, however, evangelicals who proclaim their allegiance to the Bible and defend its full authority apparently feel quite comfortable ignoring what it says in literally hundreds of verses from cover to cover about God and the poor. In many ways, the heart of the book is a plea to affluent Christians to end the scandal of largely neglecting one of the central biblical teachings. My way of doing that was to juxtapose global poverty, biblical teaching about the poor, and spreading materialism and consumerism among affluent Christians.

Another major concern of *Rich Christians* was to avoid a purely individualistic approach to the analysis and alleviation of poverty. Often evangelicals have understood sin in exclusively personal terms and neglected the clear prophetic teaching that structures themselves can be evil and unjust. I insisted that sin is both personal and social. And I argued that there were important areas of structural injustice that contributed significantly to global poverty.

And then, finally, I tried to be specific and concrete about how Christians should respond. I have little patience with people who write abstract theology or deliver theoretical sermons without applying them to the tough world where you and I must struggle with reality. So I offered concrete suggestions about how we should live simpler personal lifestyles, make our churches consistent with the fact that we worship the God of the poor, and work to correct unjust socioeconomic structures that oppress the poor.

Very briefly, that is what I tried to do. A lot of people liked the result, and a lot of people didn't! I was surprised by the positive response—and very grateful to God. To that continuing stream of people I meet on my travels who kindly thank me for the book's impact on their lives, I say, "Well, it is far easier to talk about it than to live it. So pray for me, because the book continues to be a prod and challenge to me too."

Not everybody, of course, sent flowers. There were vigorous critics. To some, I was a socialist guilt manipulator who knew nothing about economics and therefore had no clue about how to solve the problem of widespread poverty.[3]

The charge that the book was proposing a statist, socialist solution is simply wrong. Everything, of course, depends on your definition of socialism. If favoring any government intervention in the market means one is a socialist, then almost everyone, including good friends like Wheaton economist P. J. Hill, is a socialist.

I think the more useful and more widely used definition of socialism refers to a centrally planned economy where the government owns the bulk of or all of the means of production. Not a sentence in the book recommends that. I'm a Mennonite farm kid, after all. Have you ever met a Mennonite farmer who wants the government to own his land? In one section, I explicitly defend private property.

It is true that I claim that the present economic order produces some very unjust results. And at the very end of the book, I note that whereas I have advocated the reform of present structures, others are calling for far more sweeping structural change. My only further comment in the first edition is that I don't know enough to adjudicate that claim. In the second edition in 1984, I stated very explicitly that I felt the right way forward was a decentralized market economy.

It has always rather surprised me that anyone could read the book and conclude that my only concern was statist government intervention. After all, part 3, which deals with how we should respond, has three chapters. The first, chapter 7, discusses how individual persons and families should live more simply and share more generously. Chapter 8 pleads with the church to change its spending patterns. And only in the last chapter, 9, do I finally talk about what government should do.

In a moment, when I get to my reflections on how I have changed, I'll acknowledge that today I speak more positively about the market economy and am more cautious on government intervention. But the charge that *Rich Christians* was recommending socialism or Marxism was never true.

What about the charge of being a guilt manipulator? I tried hard from the first edition on to make it clear that God wants us to exult and delight in the goodness of creation. Occasionally I end up at Thanksgiving type feasts and am horrified at the way the person praying seems to feel guilty for enjoying the wonderful meal. I don't! I want to celebrate the fantastic goodness of creation by stuffing myself at Thanksgiving and Christmas dinners.

But overeating every day is sin. And so is neglecting what the Bible says about the fact that faithful Christians will share in costly ways with the poor. Worldwide today, Christians have 62 percent of the world's wealth. We devote only 3 percent of that vast wealth to charities, Christian and non-Christian, and most of that goes to ministries in our own affluent contexts. I think affluent, materialistic North American Christians who give only a fraction of a tithe to charity ought to feel guilty. According to the Bible, sin is an objective reality, and when we commit sin, our guilty consciences are God's plea to us to repent and change. Even if everything I say in the sections on structural injustice is wrong (and I don't believe that), it is still true that the neglect of the poor by affluent Christians is a damnable sin against almighty God.

A third criticism focused around the charge that I thought all poverty resulted from economic injustice and oppression and that therefore, since I did not recognize other causes, I was fundamentally misleading people about how to reduce poverty.

It is true that I talked more about what I considered economic injustices for which industrialized nations had some responsibility, than about other causes of poverty. But already in the first edition I said explicitly that third-world poverty is caused by wealthy elites in poor nations, "ancient social patterns, inherited values, and cherished philosophical perspectives," as well as by the actions of industrialized nations (p. 139). But I was writing to a Western audience, and so I emphasized where I thought we were at fault.

Another way to get at the same point is to show how the Bible talks about different causes of poverty. From the second edition on, but not in the first, I pointed out that the Bible recognized (1) voluntary poverty for the sake of the kingdom; (2) poverty that results from an individual's sinful choices (laziness, for example); (3) poverty that results from calamity; and (4) poverty that results from the oppression of others. I think those distinctions are important, and the first edition would have been better if I had included them.

I also acknowledge that I should have said more about the cultural factors (worldviews, personal character, etc.) that affect the creation of wealth. That point is not absent, even in the first edition. I pointed out (pp. 208–9) that if the masses of poor people in countries like India are to overcome poverty, then a fundamental transformation in the self-consciousness of the poor must occur. And I suggested that precisely a full communication of biblical faith with its clear teaching that God sides with the poor and hates their oppression is what the poor need. I held up as a model a holistic program in Liberia that combined evangelism and community development (pp. 186–87). By the second edition, I made even more explicit a related point that I had always believed, namely, that personal conversion through faith in Jesus Christ is the most powerful way that poor, marginalized, and humiliated people can come to a new sense of their worth, dignity, and ability to change. I don't really think I have changed my mind here at all. But I do acknowledge that emphasizing these cultural factors somewhat more would have produced a better balance.

One final area related to this third criticism pertains to the issue of the creation of wealth. My good critics have charged that I thought economics was a zero-sum game where one person's gain is necessarily another's loss. Therefore, redistribution is the only way to work at the problem of poverty. Again, I think that charge is nonsense. From the first edition on, I made strong statements about the goodness of creation and economic prosperity (pp. 127–30). I vigorously advocated focusing major economic assistance on promoting rural economic development so that the poor could be more economically productive (pp. 218–19)—that is, create wealth. And I recommended sending twice as much of our personal charitable contributions for the poor to programs of agricultural and community development as to public policy programs to change the structures of society (p. 184).

113

What about the charge that I was a naive theologian who knew nothing about economics and therefore usually got my economics wrong? Well, the first part is partly correct. I don't pretend to be a professional economist. And I probably did get the economic analysis wrong at times, especially in the first edition. In the second edition, Roland Hoksbergen, a bright young Calvin College economist, helped me avoid at least some of the earlier mistakes.

Craig Gay raises a number of interesting issues in his significant book *With Liberty and Justice for Whom? The Recent Evangelical Debate over Capitalism.*[4] Chapter 1 seems to me to mix together different authors without either adequate attention to what the individual authors themselves say in their various publications or adequate analysis of where they differ substantially from one another. Here I note just a few problems.

First, Gay fails to make the obvious and crucial distinction between the claim that some aspects of the present capitalist economy are unjust and the claim that capitalism is primarily unjust and oppressive.[5] One can argue that the present market economy produces *some* injustice and still think, as I do, that the market economy is better than any other economic system now available. If he had made that simple distinction with care, he would have had to rewrite chapter 1.

Second, the claim that the present capitalist system has resulted in a dangerous concentration of power does not mean that one wants to abolish the market economy.[6] Rather, people like me want to decentralize it so everybody has private property.

Third, the charge that people like me (or Orlando Costas, who was a missionary!) think that we change the social order "principally" through economic change[7] simply reflects a lack of knowledge about my writings of the past two decades. Gay's footnote 61[8] provides one example of his careless, distorted argument. He quotes Stephen Mott's claim that one should not limit one's concern to change society "merely" to changing individuals and then adds that "the evangelical left" critiques conservatives who see change coming "primarily" from changing individuals. All this is supposed to support his claim that "the evangelical left" is "primarily" focused on structural change! Surely Gay knows his citations simply do not logically support his argument. Gay simply ignores the third position (which I and many of the others cited in this chapter have always argued), that is, that we must have both personal conversion and structural change, and we should not say one is the principal channel of change and the other is relatively insignificant. I have been writing and speaking about this for decades; *One Sided Christianity? Uniting the Church to Heal a Lost and Broken World* published by Zondervan/Harper in 1993 is my fullest statement.[9]

Fourth, Gay says (he quotes me, but the quotation again simply does not say what he is arguing) that we claim that the denunciation of economic exploitation was "the chief concern of the prophets."[10] I have gone out of my way from the first edition of *Rich Christians* to insist that the prophets were concerned equally with economic exploitation and idolatry.

Fifth, Gay says some understand salvation socially and structurally and place little emphasis on personal salvation. There are certainly Christians who say that. But I and many of the others he cites have always explicitly and carefully rejected this mistake. This is one example of how his broad categorization and generalization in chapter 1 substantially distort the facts.

Sixth, he speculates on what "the evangelical left," because of their alleged Marxism, may do in the future—that is, abandon the biblical truth that the kingdom of God transcends this world.[11] Lacking evidence, he merely speculates. Rejecting that kind of liberalism has been central to the agenda held by me and many of the others he quotes in this chapter. This kind of gratuitous speculation is not only poor scholarship. It is unfair.

In a recent book called *Godly Materialism*, John Schneider argues that I do not understand the biblical affirmation of the goodness and abundance of material things. Schneider says he wrote largely for wealthy Christian professionals who are "financially secure, if not extremely rich, and most adopt a lifestyle that is more or less commensurate with that of the middle or upper middle class."[12] Central to Schneider's agenda is his concern to assure these people that they need not feel guilty about their affluent lifestyles. Is that really, I wonder, where Amos and Jesus would have placed the emphasis?

Schneider attacks what he calls my allegedly "utilitarian reasoning," saying, "That is in essence the view that enjoyment of superfluous wealth is morally wrong in a context where others have unsatisfied basic needs."[13] Well, I guess I plead guilty to thinking that enjoying superfluous wealth while others are starving is wrong. That does not mean that our sharing with the poor means that we, too, must live in poverty. Nor does it mean that we should agonize over every daily expenditure. And, yes, we will have to wrestle with the little word *superfluous*.

Unlike Schneider, I think the general distinction between necessities and luxuries is helpful. Granted, the distinction is not easy to make. I understand necessities to include what we need to participate in our society in a joyful, dignified way. And that includes times of "luxurious" celebration. But if we are not living significantly differently—and sharing more generously—than the rest of our affluent neighbors, I wonder if we have really listened either to Jesus or to the poor.

When one gets serious about living more simply in order to share generously for the sake of evangelism and justice, a difficult problem does emerge. How much should I spend on myself? There is no neat formula, no legalistic calculus, for answering that question. What I always suggest to people at that point is a process: read all the Bible says, study the needs of the poor and the unevangelized, discuss your family budget with a few trusted friends, and pray hard, asking the Spirit to show you what to share. Then make a plan, live that way for a year or two, and then reevaluate. Meanwhile, give generously, revel in the material world, and certainly don't feel guilty when you celebrate at Christmas.

I admit that ambiguity remains. I acknowledge that I continue to puzzle (and sometimes really struggle) over whether this fishing equipment or that vacation is justified. But if Schneider thinks he has escaped that dilemma, then either he is kidding himself or he does *really* mean that we should enjoy whatever luxuries we can afford no matter how many people are starving.

So much for my critics. I want to turn next to reflect on some areas where my thoughts have changed.

I think that the most significant change relates to chapter 4 of *Rich Christians*. One of my arguments there was that God is opposed to "extremes of wealth" (p. 90) and therefore God has ordained mechanisms among his redeemed people (Israel and the church) to prevent "great economic inequality" (p. 88). In the 1990 edition, I was more cautious, saying God disapproved of "great extremes of wealth" (p. 67) or, in another place, "scandalous extremes of wealth and poverty" (71–72) among God's redeemed people.

All that, of course, is rather vague. What we need to know is the biblical definition of equity or equality. I finally got around to thinking about that with some care in print in an article I did for *Interpretation* published in 1989 under the title "Toward a Biblical Perspective on Equality."[14] Unfortunately, there is no biblical passage that offers an answer to this question in a comprehensive systematic way. We must piece together vast amounts of biblical material to develop a biblical paradigm on equality.

I believe that biblical revelation clearly supports equality before the law. I also believe that biblical revelation clearly does not teach the notion of absolute equality of outcome for income and wealth (i.e., every person must enjoy exactly the same amount of economic resources). What then is the biblical ideal of equity with regard to economic resources?

The biblical material points to two things: (1) It requires equality of economic opportunity up to the point where all persons have access to the capital (land, knowledge, money, etc.) necessary to be able to earn a decent living so they can live as dignified members of their social community. (2) For those who are truly unable because of disability, or whatever, to care for themselves, the Bible demands equality of economic outcome (via some kind of transfer) up to the point where the disabled, widows, and others who are at risk have the basic necessities essential for a decent life in their society.

Today I do not believe, as I probably did in 1976, that great differences of wealth are inherently evil even when that wealth has been earned justly, is now being used wisely and compassionately, and the owners are not living an extravagant personal lifestyle. What I want to know is what the differing ratios between rich and poor do to the people on the bottom. Let's imagine a situation where increasing the differential between the richest 15 percent and the poorest 15 percent from 5 to 1 to 10 to 1 actually also improved the lot of the poorest 15 percent by 100 percent, whereas reducing the differential from 5 to 1 to 2 to 1 actually did nothing to increase the economic well-being of the poorest. I would clearly consider the former change morally better, even though the gap between the richest and poorest increased. I think biblical faith compels us to use as one of our central criteria for measuring societies and their proposals for change the question: What does it do to the poorest, the weakest, the most marginalized?

The Christian doctrine of sin compels me to add a major qualification to the argument of the preceding paragraph—that is, that great inequalities of wealth do not matter if that wealth was acquired justly and is being used justly to improve the lot of the poorest. Biblical revelation and human history show that power tends to corrupt. Great inequalities of power produce enormous temptation to sin for both the very powerful and the very weak. That does not mean that equality of income is the ideal, but it does mean that great extremes of wealth bring powerful temptations.

One might argue that my claim that the Bible demands equality of economic opportunity up to the point of everyone enjoying the capital to be able to earn a decent living is a very modest claim. That may be true. But just reaching that goal today for minorities in our country and for the poor around the world would require dramatic change. We don't even have anything approaching equality of educational opportunity in this country, much less in the rest of the world. Think of how different our world would be if every single person and family had the opportunity to possess land—had the knowledge or money they needed to work so they could earn a living that enabled them to have the basic necessities of life and be dignified, participating members of their community!

I believe biblical revelation summons us to work vigorously to implement that vision of equality.[15]

Second, today I also would restate my exegesis of the Jubilee passage in Leviticus 25, at least at one point. I'm not sure it is clarifying to speak of land returning to the original owners "without compensation" (p. 88). The text of Leviticus 25 on the Jubilee makes it clear that the new owner pays for the number of crops between the purchase date and the time of the next Jubilee. The longer the time till that next Jubilee, the higher the price. The purchaser really acquires the right to the intervening crops, not unlimited, unending ownership. Therefore, to speak of the land returning to the original owner "without compensation" is confusing. It is not accurate to suggest that the original owner got something for nothing. He got precisely what he bargained for—namely, the loss of his crops for a specified period in exchange for cash.

At the same time, it is very important to see that the whole structure of the Jubilee is designed to guard against more and more centralized economic power and wealth whereby some people lose their productive capital forever. The text is clearly in favor of promoting a decentralized economy in which everybody has the productive resources to earn their own way, and therefore nobody need be in poverty. In that important sense, this text opposes ever-growing extremes of wealth and poverty. Private property and the ability to create the wealth needed for a decent life are so good that God wants everybody to have some!

Third, I would not be as critical of capitalism as I was in the first edition (p. 114). Today I would argue—as I already did in the 1984 edition (pp. 104, 253) and even more clearly in the 1990 edition (pp. 88–89, 213)—that the market economy is a better basic framework for the economic order than any alternative we know.

I did not say that clearly in the first edition. I do today. But it is important to see carefully what I was trying to critique in the first edition.

First, precisely as I affirmed the importance of private property, I rejected as unbiblical the notion that the right of private property is absolute. I still think that the Bible says that God alone is the absolute owner (p. 115). Leviticus 25:25-28 teaches that the right of the original owner to have his land back (if he regained solvency before the next Jubilee) was a higher right than the new purchaser's claims.

Second, I was concerned to reject the notion that the maximization of profits is the highest good (p. 114). Persons matter more than things. Businesses need to make a profit to survive. But to elevate maximization of profits to the highest priority, ignoring the needs of people, is to fall into blasphemous idolatry.

Third, I believed then (and still do, although some of my examples may have been wrong) that the current operations of our capitalist economy sometimes produce substantial injustice. It is precisely because I believe in searching for a careful, accurate analysis of how much that is true that I am currently engaged in the Oxford conference on Christian faith and economics.[16]

Today I would add a couple additional points. If you start at any given moment in history and operate a totally laissez-faire economy (i.e., with no government intervention), and if, as is always the case, some people at that moment lack the capital necessary to earn their own way (e.g., former slaves immediately after emancipation), then you have injustice built into the system. Furthermore, there is always the great danger that sinful people (and that means all of us) who acquire great economic power in a market economy will abuse that power in a variety of unjust ways to protect and further our self-interest.

None of these points leads me to conclude that we ought to prefer socialism, even democratic socialism. I think the basic market framework is preferable. Therefore, I favor and work for a democratic political order and a market economy as the best currently available overall political-economic framework. At the same time, I conclude that under some circumstances, some government intervention in the economy is warranted, wise, and just.

That comment leads me to the fourth area where I have changed. I am more cautious and more skeptical about government intervention today than earlier. Good friends like P. J. Hill have helped me see that with disturbing frequency government bureaucracy and regulation mess things up more than they make things better. So I would demand more supporting data today before recommending government intervention.

Sometimes, however, government intervention is needed and wise. My examples would include environmental legislation that forces all companies to pay the full costs of pollution so that gross polluters do not enjoy a competitive advantage; a carbon tax on fossil fuels, which then uses the market mechanism for its basic implementation; outright grants to college students from poor homes. The last point illustrates the kind of government intervention I support. It empowers the poor by providing lifelong capital (knowledge in an information society). Thus it enables them to earn their own way rather than build dependency à la the welfare system. Such grants operate with a minimum of bureaucracy, and they require work and responsibility (if you don't study, you lose the grant within a semester).

I would offer several questions that should be asked of any proposal for government intervention in the market economy. First, does it genuinely empower the poorest and weakest members of society so they have new opportunity to earn their own way? Second, does it decrease or increase the centralization of power? (I find it puzzling and ironic that some conservatives clearly—and correctly!—perceive the danger of centralized power in centrally planned, state-owned economies, but fail to see the danger of centralized economic power wielded by huge multinational corporations whose vast economic clout sometimes enables them to dominate the media and politics.) Third, will it work? Does it actually accomplish what it proposes, or will its unintended, negative side effects outweigh any actual benefits?

I think many of the most interesting and significant debates about economics today come just at this point. Precisely what kind of and how much government intervention within the basic market economy will successfully and efficiently empower the poor and decentralize power? I'm as upset as anyone else about silly government interventions that are counterproductive. We need to invest a lot more energy in working together across ideological lines to develop hard-nosed evaluations of proposed government interventions so that we only do those things that have a reasonable chance of improving our common life.

It should be clear from the above that I still think (as does, for example, my good friend John Perkins) that the right kind of redistribution is a biblical imperative. Voluntary redistribution is in many ways preferable to state-mandated redistribution. If God demands that God's people share God's special concern for the poor, and if God demands that all have equality of economic opportunity to the degree specified above, then we clearly sin against almighty God if we as wealthy Christians do not share in costly ways that truly empower the poor to earn their own way. That is why I so enthusiastically support Christian business leaders like David Bussau who are actively promoting small loans for microeconomic development among the poor.[17]

At the same time, I believe there is a *limited* role for government here as well.[18] It must be done in ways that avoid dangerously centralized political power. It must be efficient. It must not harm the economy with the result that everyone, especially the poorest, lose jobs and become worse off than before. It must be done in a democratic way. Again, the grants to poor college students illustrate the kind of proposal I would support. The basic purpose of government-operated redistribution must be to provide for the poorest members of society the opportunity to possess the resources to earn their own way. In fact, I like very much the way conservative economist Amy Sherman states it in her recent book, *Preferential Option*: "Interventions by the state designed to protect society's most vulnerable members, enhance their 'human capital' or increase their access to property rights . . . are affirmed. The neoliberal approach insists, however, that such 'welfare'-oriented polices be judged on the basis of their actual results in improving the lives of intended beneficiaries. Lofty rhetoric and good intentions are not enough."[19] I agree—vigorously!

My thinking has changed somewhat in a variety of other, less significant areas as well. I'll mention just three in passing. My wife, Arbutus, and I discovered that as our children became teenagers and then college students, we needed to modify the way we calculated what I called the graduated tithe for our giving. But we still use it and find it helpful. Second, I still think that American individualism has blinded us to the powerful biblical call for extensive mutuality and sacrificial sharing (including economic sharing within the body of Christ). But I would today qualify the first edition's language about "unlimited liability" and "complete availability" to other sisters and brothers (pp. 97, 101, 103). Finally, the second and third editions dropped the apocalyptic scenario of nuclear wars of redistribution. As I grow older, I find myself wanting to be more careful not to suggest that the world will soon self-destruct in cataclysmic convulsion unless people instantly resolve the problems just outlined in my most recent book.

Yes, I have changed my mind at some points. In a couple of instances, I think the changes are substantial. Knowing that I am both very finite and also sinful, I hope and pray that I can continue learning from others, including my critics, until I pass on to that more blessed life in the presence of the risen Lord where our insight is no longer biased and imperfect.

Finally, some brief comments about the future. First, the fundamental problem is still with us. People are starving, and we are largely unconcerned in spite of what the Bible says. One hundred thousand people die each day of starvation, malnutrition, and related diseases. Over the last twenty years, we have made some progress in literacy training, immunization of children against disease, and reduction of the rate of population growth. But over a billion[20] of the world's people still live in desperate poverty with virtually no education, health care, or even enough protein and other food to develop healthy bodies. That translates into massive global pain and anguish that could largely be prevented.

Furthermore, I fear that self-preoccupied materialism and consumerism have grown worse in North American evangelical circles in the years since I wrote the first edition. Maybe—in fact, I hope—I am wrong. One way to check would be to survey the graduates from the business programs of Christian colleges over the last twenty years to discover how many have gone into business to empower the poor and how many have been primarily concerned to acquire affluence for themselves.

Equally clear is the fact that biblical teaching about God's concern for the poor and demand for just social structures has not changed. No matter how evangelical we claim our theology to be, if we do not make God's concern for the poor as central to our thinking and living as the Bible does, we are heretical Christians in great danger of someday hearing Jesus' terrible words "Depart from me." Meanwhile, our combination of astounding affluence and self-centered neglect of the poor undercuts our evangelism, prompts secular people to mock our religious hypocrisy, and disgraces the God we worship.

Second, we must honestly face the fact that the present economic order is not working well for substantial numbers of people. Millions in our cities have no reasonable hope that they will ever have the opportunity for a quality education, a good job, and a decent house. Hundreds of millions of people in Latin America, Africa, and Asia are not benefiting from our global market economy. I don't agree with those who claim that correcting those problems is impossible within the framework of a market economy. But unless all of us who think that democratic capitalism can solve such problems honestly face the full depth and extent of the agony and suffering that the present economic structures tolerate and foster, we are simply dishonest. And unless we then engage in costly sacrificial action that corrects those problems, we are unchristian.

Third, I think we need to work even harder than in the past to create contexts for open, honest dialogue about the genuine differences that exist among us. If we disagree about the various causes of poverty and their relative weight, then the way to make progress is not by throwing ideological bricks at each other. Rather, it is by sitting down together, especially within the body of Christ, in openness to biblical revelation and the concrete factual data, to see precisely where we disagree and how those disagreements can be adjudicated. I am as eager as anyone else to avoid exaggerating the extent to which North American activities (both public and private) contribute to poverty in Latin America, Africa, or Asia. Let's humbly sort through the data together.

Fourth, let's get on with what we already know works. We know that microenterprise development among the poor empowers the poor to create wealth in highly successful ways. We know that private agencies usually do a better job of efficiently and effectively sharing resources with the poor than do government programs. We know that holistic ministries that combine evangelism and church planting with economic development produce more lasting change than economic programs by themselves. And we know that all these things are costly in terms of both our budgets and our time. So let's dare to live sacrificial lifestyles that share resources with the poor in ways that empower them to become dignified, participating members of society.

A little more than twenty years ago, Wayne Gordon, a boy from Iowa, came to Wheaton College. After graduation, God called Gordon and his wife to live in a very poor section of Chicago. In spite of repeated break-ins at their home and dangers of many kinds, they loved inner-city youth and led them to Christ. But "Gordie" knew that God cared for the whole person, so he developed a medical clinic with fourteen doctors, a housing program that renovates low-income housing, and a superb educational program for inner-city youth.

At the same time, Gordie did not merely renovate housing and develop job-training programs. He built a community of Christians that discipled new converts, developed believers with strong Christian character, and nurtured stable Christian families that in turn attracted more people to accept Christ. Staff in the community center eagerly share Christ. Today Lawndale Church has about five hundred members, and its community center (with its annual seven-million-dollar budget) is a wonderful illustration of effective holistic mission. In fact, last year they led a hundred people to Christ.

That is the kind of combination of evangelism and social transformation that I believe in. That is what I plead for in my most recent books, *One-Sided Christianity?* and *Cup of Water, Bread of Life*. And it works too. But it is costly.

I end with a question: Why do Christian colleges produce only a handful of Wayne Gordons every decade? If our evangelical colleges were faithfully presenting the whole gospel, including what it says about God's special concern for the poor, and evangelical students were truly listening to the Word and the Spirit, would there not be hundreds of African American, Hispanic, Asian, and white graduates every year who would leave their halls to do the same kind of thing Wayne Gordon has done in the inner cities of America and the world?

Notes

1. A portion of the lecture was published in *Discernment*, Spring 1995, 2–3, 6–7.

2. Ronald J. Sider, *Rich Christians in an Age of Hunger*, 1st ed. (Downers Grove, IL: Inter-Varsity, 1977); 2nd ed. (Downers Grove, IL: Inter-Varsity, 1984); 3rd ed. (Dallas: W. Publishing Group, 1990); 4th ed. (Nashville, TN: Thomas Nelson, 1997); 5th ed. (Nashville, TN: Thomas Nelson, 2005); 6th ed. (Nashville, TN: Thomas Nelson, 2015).

3. For example, David Chilton, *Productive Christians in an Age of Guilt Manipulators* (Tyler, TX: Institute for Christian Economics, 1981).

4. Craig Gay, *With Liberty and Justice for Whom? The Recent Evangelical Debate over Capitalism* (Grand Rapids: Eerdmans, 1991).

5. Gay, 22.

6. Gay, 25.

7. Gay, 34.

8. Gay, 34–35.

9. Baker later republished it under the title *Good News and Good Works: A Theology for the Whole Gospel.*

10. Gay, *With Liberty and Justice,* 7.

11. Gay, 62–63.

12. John Schneider, *Godly Materialism: Rethinking Money and Possessions* (Downers Grove, IL: InterVarsity, 1994), 14.

13. Schneider, 171.

14. Ronald J. Sider, "Toward a Biblical Perspective on Equality," *Interpretation,* April 1989, 156–69.

15. That is basically what I advocated at the end of the first edition, where I pleaded for a change to "enable everyone to earn a just living" (p. 223). See also p. 116, where I stated the ideal of each family possessing "the means to earn its own way."

16. I served as general secretary of the international process (1987–95) and conferences that produced the Oxford Declaration on Christian Faith and Economics. See Herbert Schlossberg, Vinay Samuel, and Ronald J. Sider, eds., *Christianity and Economics in the Post–Cold War Era: The Oxford Declaration and Beyond* (Grand Rapids: Eerdmans, 1994).

17. See chapter 7 of my *Cup of Water, Bread of Life: Inspiring Stories about Overcoming Lopsided Christianity* (Grand Rapids: Zondervan, 1994) for a discussion of Bussau.

18. Both the Jubilee text, which describes a structural mechanism that God wants God's people to maintain and the many clear texts about the king's responsibility to promote *mishphat* and *tsedaqah* (which include both legal and economic components) support this role for government. For example, Psalms 45:4-5; 72; 101:8; Jeremiah 21:12; 22:15-16.

19. Amy L. Sherman, *Preferential Option: A Christian and Neoliberal Strategy for Latin Americas' Poor* (Grand Rapids: Eerdmans, 1992), 7.

20. See Bread for the World's fifth annual report, *Hunger 1995: Causes of Hunger* (Silver Spring, MD: Bread for the World Institute, 1994), 2.

CHAPTER 8

Why Would Anybody Ever Want to Be an Evangelical?

I first gave this speech at Colorado College, Colorado Springs, Colorado, on January 22, 1994. This speech was part of a four-day all-college symposium on spirituality and religion, which featured a wide range of speakers representing very diverse views, including New Age ideology, feminist spirituality, Native American religious views, and more. Speakers included Vanderbilt University political scientist Jean Bethke Elshtain, Harvard Divinity School professor Elisabeth Schüssler Fiorenza, and Catholic sociologist Andrew Greeley. I presented this speech at least seven more times in the next ten-plus years in the United States and Canada.

Today evangelicals represent a somewhat smaller percentage of the total population than in 1994, although they still are a major group in American society. Unfortunately, the majority of evangelicals have become even more politically conservative and right-wing than in 1994—a reality that was exceedingly clear during the presidency of Donald Trump.

Aren't evangelicals the folks who bring us TV evangelists with their sex scandals? Aren't evangelicals right-wing fanatics and gun-toting NRA members who fight all sensible gun control? Aren't evangelicals anti-feminist reactionaries who want their women in the kitchen, submissive, barefoot, and pregnant? Don't they want to take away the civil rights of gay Americans? And aren't they intellectual obscurantists who reject modern science? Don't they destroy the environment because they think the world is going to end very soon, so we might as well use all we can before God blows it to bits?

The public image of evangelicals is not very good. At worst, evangelicals are seen by many Americans as dangerous threats to freedom, justice, or the environment. At best, as naive, reactionary folk who want to return to the Middle Ages. Or silly, superstitious legalists.

The popular stereotype of evangelicals, however, is far too simplistic. Some evangelicals fit the stereotype. But I also am an evangelical, and I don't fit that image.

I'm a feminist. I defend civil rights for gay Americans. I support vigorous gun control legislation. I'm the leader of a Christian environmental organization. I have worked hard for justice for the poor and for nuclear disarmament. In fact, I debated Jerry Falwell on the nuclear freeze issue in the early '80s. I was in favor of a nuclear freeze; Jerry opposed it!

The widespread stereotype that all evangelicals are right-wing fanatics is simply wrong. Well then, who are the evangelicals?

First of all, they are a big group. A 1992 Gallup poll estimated that evangelicals make up 38 percent of the American population. A very careful study by four political scientists in 1992 discovered that there are almost exactly as many evangelicals in the United States as Catholics: each are about 23 percent of the total population. That translates into 43 million voters.[1]

What do these folks believe? Their core beliefs include the following:

1. The historic Christian affirmations about Jesus of Nazareth are true. Jesus is true God as well as true man, the only Savior, who died for our sins and rose again from the dead.

2. The Old Testament and New Testament are a special, authoritative revelation from God and the final source for what we should believe and how we should act.

3. Telling others about Jesus Christ and inviting others to follow him are a central part of Christian faith.

Beyond some core beliefs that all evangelicals share, there is much diversity in church life and political viewpoints. I will illustrate this by using the 1992 study by the political scientists I mentioned earlier.

Most, although not all, evangelicals are pro-life and oppose abortion. Virtually all evangelicals believe homosexual practice is contrary to God's will. But the political scientists found that a majority of evangelicals also favor a number of political stands that are usually identified as progressive or liberal rather than conservative. A majority of evangelicals favor national health insurance, good government programs to reduce poverty, and environmental initiatives.

Evangelicals have had bad press. The stereotypes don't fit many of us. I invite you to set aside those defective images, if only for this lecture, and explore with me in a little detail what evangelicals believe and do and why they think and do that.

Of necessity, I must sketch a broad outline. I'm aware that every sentence needs a book (or ten) to substantiate the claims being made.

Evangelical Christians believe that many modern thinkers have committed intellectual suicide. Modern folk claim that people, indeed all living things, are merely the product of a blind materialistic process governed by chance. Modern science, they claim, proves that. That is the viewpoint that still dominates the universities, the media, and the intelligentsia generally. I have recently been involved in a major project on the environment with Carl Sagan and others. Carl Sagan illustrates this huge mistake of modern thinkers. At the beginning of his book *Cosmos*, Sagan says nature is all that is, was, and ever shall be.[2]

Notice what follows if they are right. If everything results from matter and chance, then truth and ethics do not exist. People are simply sophisticated materialistic machines. Ethical values are totally subjective, merely an expression of our individual feelings.

In fact, Bertrand Russell said that those who have the best poison gas will determine the ethics of the future. Ethics is what the powerful say is right. According to Marxist ethics, whatever serves the interest of the party is true and good. Human life is not sacred and can be destroyed at society's convenience. If this supposedly "scientific" view is correct, then truth and ethics are illusions. Persons are machines. Truth, justice, freedom, responsibility, and liberty disappear. Society self-destructs.

Christians have a radically different view of the world. We believe that all life is the creation of a loving, personal God, although, of course, God may have used a complex evolutionary process to do that. Human beings are free, responsible persons whose deepest joy and ultimate obligation is to live in right relationship with their loving Creator. Created in God's image, every human being has ultimate value. Ethical values are an expression of the very nature of God, not a relativistic product of a blind materialistic process.

Christians have believed these things for centuries. How did the modern secular view arise? It arose in the eighteenth century when more and more thinkers mistakenly concluded that one could not believe in both modern science and miracles at the same time. Consequently, modern thinkers rejected the view held by Christians for eighteen hundred years that Jesus is true God and that he rose from the dead. They abandoned the belief that persons are created in the image of God and called to respond to God and live forever in God's presence. Instead, they saw people as complex machines produced by a blind materialistic process and destined to decay and disappear like the grass, the worms, and the trees.

Understanding this basic mistake in modern thought is crucial. It is sheer confusion to suppose that more and more scientific information makes belief in God the Creator or belief in miracles more and more intellectually irresponsible. Science simply tells us with greater and greater precision what nature regularly does. In principle, no amount of scientific information could ever tell us whether there might or might not be a God who exists outside of nature. Now, of course, if an all-powerful God exists outside nature, that God could intervene in nature any time God chose. Does such a being exist?

One way to look for an answer to that question is to ask whether there is any evidence that points to the existence of such a God. I was trained at Yale as a historian. As a historian, I think the historical evidence we have about Jesus of Nazareth points in that direction.

Over the centuries, Christians have claimed two very unusual things about Jesus: (1) in addition to being a great ethical teacher, he was also God in the flesh; (2) after being crucified, he returned to life after three days.

If modern thinkers are right, if blind materialistic process is all there is, then resurrection from the dead is impossible. But if God exists, then resurrection from the dead would be possible—anytime God chose to do that. If really good historical evidence existed to show that Jesus was truly alive on the third day, that would also strongly suggest that God exists.

Interestingly, Anthony Flew said something similar a few years ago. Flew, as you know, is one of the great modern philosophers. For decades he was also a prominent atheist. But listen to what Flew said about Jesus' resurrection: "We are agreed that the question of whether Jesus did rise from the dead is of supreme theoretical and practical importance. For the knowable fact that he did, if indeed it is a knowable fact, is the best if not the only reason for accepting that Jesus is the God of Abraham, Isaac and Israel."[3] Well, what evidence is there?

Before we investigate the historical evidence for Jesus' resurrection, however, I want to sketch two other important historical facts about Jesus of Nazareth.

First, Jesus was a radical guy. He challenged the status quo of his time in all kinds of ways. Jesus shocked the rich with his words about sharing. He told the rich young man who came inquiring about eternal life (and probably about membership in Jesus' new circle as well) that he would have to sell his vast holdings and give all his wealth to the poor. Jesus urged the rich to make loans to the poor, even if there was no reasonable hope of repayment (Luke 6:34-35). Those who do not feed the hungry and clothe the naked, he said, go to hell (Matthew 25:31-46).

Jesus' special concern for the poor extended to all the marginalized, weak, and socially ostracized. In sharp contrast to his contemporaries, Jesus demonstrated a special interest in the disabled, children, prostitutes, and lepers (cf. Luke 7:32-50; 17:11-19). In Jesus' day, lepers experienced terrible ostracism, living alone in awful poverty, shouting, "Unclean, unclean!" lest anyone accidentally touch them. Jesus gently touched the lepers and miraculously healed them (Mark 1:41).

From the Dead Sea Scrolls, we learn that the Essenes, a Jewish religious group of Jesus' day, actually excluded the disabled from their religious community. Jesus, by contrast, commands the members of his new messianic community to invite precisely these people: "When you give a banquet, invite the poor, the crippled, the lame, the blind" (Luke 14:13, NIV).

Jesus' attitude toward women reflects the same sweeping challenge to the status quo. In Jesus' day, it was a scandal for a man to appear in public with a woman. A woman's word was considered useless in court. It was better to burn a copy of the Torah (the first five books of the Hebrew Bible) than to allow a woman to touch it. Indeed, one first-century religious leader said that teaching one's daughter Torah was like teaching her lechery. Women were excluded from most parts of the temple. Nor did they count in calculating the quorum needed for a meeting in the synagogue. First-century Jewish men regularly thanked God that they were not Gentiles, slaves, or women.

Jesus and his new community rejected centuries of male prejudice and treated women as equals. Jesus appeared with women in public (John 4:27) and taught them theology (Luke 10:38-42). He allowed a woman that everybody knew was a sinner to wash his feet with her tears, wipe them with her long hair, and kiss and perfume them—all in public (Luke 7:36-50)! Absolutely scandalous! When Mary abandoned her traditional role of cooking food to listen to Jesus' theology lesson, Martha objected. But Jesus defended Mary (Luke 10:38-42). Jesus rejected Moses' teaching on divorce, which allowed a man (but not a woman) to dismiss his spouse if she did not find favor in his eyes (Deuteronomy 24:1-4). Jesus called both husband and wife to live together in lifelong covenant (Mark 10:1-12). It was surely no accident that Jesus granted the first resurrection appearance to women!

Jesus must have infuriated King Herod. When someone warned him that Herod wanted to kill him, Jesus shot back his response: "Go tell that fox . . ." (Luke 13:32). In Jesus' day, that word meant about the same thing as the slang use of the word *skunk* does today.

Perhaps most radical of all, Jesus said his followers should love their enemies. Jesus taught and lived a radical ethic that deeply challenged the status quo. That alone probably would have been enough to get him put away.

But Jesus did another thing. He made outrageous claims about himself. He claimed divine authority to forgive sins. The religious leaders rightly said that only God could do that. Jesus placed his own authority above that of Moses. And at his trial, he acknowledged that he was the Son of God.

So Jesus got killed for two reasons! First, because he was a dangerous social radical. Second, because they said he was a blasphemer who claimed to be the only Son of God.

So he was crucified. And that would seem to have put an end to Jesus. Except for one thing. Soon after his death, there were reports that he was alive again.

Now, as I said, I am a historian. I did my doctoral work in history at Yale. I am as skeptical as you are about silly claims with no evidence. Is there any solid evidence that this carpenter from Nazareth was really alive on the third day?

I have examined the historical evidence carefully. Thousands of articles and hundreds of books have been written on the resurrection. Here I can only summarize my research in four quick points: (1) the change in the discouraged disciples; (2) the empty tomb; (3) the fact that the first witnesses were women; and (4) the very early evidence given in 1 Corinthians 15.

A short time after the crucifixion, the disciples announced to a Jerusalem crowd that Jesus had been raised from the dead. Within a few years, these same people proceeded to crisscross the eastern part of the Roman Empire, braving intense persecution and eventually experiencing martyrdom. And it was these very same people who had scattered at Jesus' arrest and fled home in despair.

What gave rise to the "resurrection faith" and the disciples' willingness to risk their lives to spread it? Professor Reginald H. Fuller, formerly of New York's Union Theological Seminary, has underlined the fact that this total transformation demands explanation: "Even the most skeptical historian has to postulate an 'X,' as M.

Dibelius called it, to account for the complete change in the behavior of the disciples, who at Jesus' arrest had fled and scattered to their own homes, but who in a few weeks were boldly preaching their message to the very people who had sought to crush the movement launched by Jesus."[4]

Professor Pinchas Lapide, a prominent European Jewish scholar, makes the same point in a recent book, *The Resurrection of Jesus.* Lapide is not a Christian, but he does believe Jesus was alive on the third day:

> I am completely convinced that the twelve from Galilee, who were all farmers, shepherds and fishermen—there was not a single theology professor to be found among them—were totally unimpressed by scholarly theologoumena, as Karl Rahner and Rudolph Bultmann write them. If they, through such a concrete historical event as the crucifixion, were so totally in despair and crushed, as all four evangelists report to us, then no less concrete a historical event was needed in order to bring them out of the deep valley of their despair and within a short time transform them into a community of salvation rejoicing to the high heavens.[5]

Lapide also writes,

> When this scared, frightened band of the apostles which was just about to throw away everything in order to flee in despair to Galilee; when these peasants, shepherds and fishermen who betrayed and denied their master and then failed him miserably, suddenly could be changed overnight into a confident mission society convinced of salvation and able to work with much more success after Easter than before Easter, then no vision or hallucination is sufficient to explain such a revolutionary transformation.[6]

The explanation of the people closest to the events was that Jesus of Nazareth arose from the tomb and appeared to them over a period of a number of days.

If one rejects the New Testament explanation of the resurrection faith and the transformation it caused in extremely discouraged people, then one is left with the very difficult task of proposing other grounds adequate to explain it. The late Robert Grant, a professor at the University of Chicago, has said, "The origin of Christianity is almost incomprehensible unless such an event took place."[7]

Second, and very important, is the question of the empty tomb. A short time after the resurrection, Peter claimed that Jesus arose from the dead and—note—he made the claim in Jerusalem. It is exceedingly significant that the controversy over the resurrection, and the rise of the first Christian church, took place precisely in Jerusalem where anybody could have gone to visit the place of burial. It was in Jerusalem that hundreds became Christians within months of Jesus' death. Obviously, it was in the interests of the religious leaders to produce the body of Jesus or give clear evidence of its proper disposal. But the earliest counterargument against the claim that Jesus was alive was the suggestion that the disciples had stolen the body. This was an acknowledgment that they could not produce the body.

Numerous attempts have been made to explain the empty tomb. The stolen-body theory is no longer accepted. It has been suggested that the Romans or the Jewish leaders removed the body before the women arrived; but, if so, the Jewish leaders would surely have conducted guided tours to the real burial place as soon as the silly disciples claimed Jesus had risen.

In his discussion of Jesus' resurrection, German theologian Professor Wolfhart Pannenberg quotes Paul Althaus to underline this point:

Paul Althaus has rightly seen this point: "In Jerusalem, the place of Jesus' execution and grave, it was proclaimed not long after his death that he had been raised. The situation *demands* that within the circle of the first community one had a reliable testimony for the fact that the grave had been found empty. The resurrection kerygma could not have been maintained in Jerusalem for a single day, for a single hour, if the emptiness of the tomb had not been established as a fact for all concerned."[8]

Since, then, the Christians and those who disagreed with them both agreed that the tomb was empty, it seems very likely that the empty tomb is a historical fact.

Third, the fact that women were the first people to visit the tomb and allegedly see the risen Jesus speaks in favor of the authenticity of the accounts. Professor C. F. D. Moule of Cambridge University has pointed out that women were notoriously invalid witnesses according to Jewish principles of evidence.[9] If, then, the early Christians had fabricated the accounts of the first visit to the tomb and the first meeting with the risen Jesus, they would certainly have claimed that men were the first witnesses. The best explanation for the priority of the women is that it actually happened that way.

Finally, we must look at the oldest evidence for the resurrection. In his first letter to the Corinthian church (the date is about AD 50–55), Paul wrote,

I delivered to you as of first importance what I also received, that Christ died for our sins in accordance with the Scriptures, that he was buried, that he was raised on the third day in accordance with the Scriptures, and that he appeared to Cephas, then to the twelve. Then he appeared to more than five hundred brethren at one time, most of whom are still alive, though some have fallen asleep. Then he appeared to James, then to all the apostles. Last of all . . . he appeared also to me. (1 Corinthians 15:3-7, RSV)

Paul implied that if his readers did not believe him, they could check, for many of the eyewitnesses were still around. In fact, the eyewitnesses on both sides saw the rapid spread of Christianity from Jerusalem to Rome.

The most important aspect of this passage, however, is its early date. Many scholars have pointed out that the words used here ("delivered" and "received") are technical terms used to refer to the well-developed Jewish practice of carefully handing down oral tradition. Paul apparently taught this to all the churches. Furthermore, Paul said he received it presumably soon after he became a Christian, in about AD 35, just a few years after Jesus' death. That means that this witness to Jesus' resurrection received a fixed form very soon after the actual events (quite possibly before Paul's first post-conversion visit to Jerusalem about AD 36 [Galations 1:18–19]).

As a historian, I find the evidence for the resurrection surprisingly strong. The most unbiased historical conclusion is that Jesus was probably alive on the third day.

How did that happen? Obviously, you and I cannot do that sort of thing even with all our modern technology. The first Christians said that God raised Jesus from the dead. That seems to me to be the most reasonable explanation. The resurrection suggests that the Christian view of the world, not the modern secular one, is true.

The resurrection is central to both what Christians think and what they do at all kinds of points. I mention briefly three implications of Jesus' resurrection.

First, the resurrection radically transformed what Jesus' followers thought about Jesus himself. Before the resurrection, Jesus' followers called him Master, Rabbi, Teacher. Afterward they called him Messiah, Son of God, Lord. This word *Lord* (Gk., *kurios*) is very important. *Kurios* was used in the Greek translation of the Old Testament to translate the word *Jahweh*. It is the word that became one of the most frequently used titles for the man from Nazareth. In Philippians 2 Paul applied to Jesus the words from Isaiah 45:23, which the monotheistic prophet had used for Jahweh. After mocking the idols, Jahweh insisted in Isaiah 45:23 that he alone was God: "To me every knee shall bow, every tongue shall swear" (Isaiah 45:23, RSV). The rabbinically trained Paul took those words from the mouth of Jahweh and applied them to Jesus, declaring that "at the name of Jesus every knee should bow, in heaven and on earth and under the earth, and every tongue confess that Jesus Christ is Lord" (Philippians 2:10-11, RSV).

It is just here that modern folk take offense. Almost everyone is happy to acknowledge Jesus as the greatest prophet of all time, the most profound ethical teacher of human history. But Christians persist in pointing out that he is true God as well as true man. That offends. Christians remember the words "I am the way, and the truth, and the life; no one comes to the Father, but by me" (John 14:6, RSV). That offends.

If Jesus was God in the flesh, then I cannot pick and choose among Jesus' teachings, accepting the things I like and rejecting those that don't feel good. Instead, I must joyfully accept him as Lord of all of my life: my politics, my economics, and my sexual life.

But Jesus taught some pretty costly things about sharing with the poor, loving my enemies, and keeping my marriage covenant for life. And I often find it hard to do what he said.

It's just at this point that a second implication of Jesus' resurrection is so important. The New Testament says that when people believe in Jesus Christ, then the same divine power that raised

Jesus from the dead now works in believers to empower them to live the way Jesus did (Ephesians 1:19-20).

Just as Christ died and was raised, so by faith we can die to the old life of selfishness and rise to a new life in Christ. Paul wrote, "We were buried therefore with [Christ] by baptism into death, so that as Christ was raised from the dead by the glory of the Father, we too might walk in newness of life" (Romans 6:4, RSV). Or as Paul put it in Galatians, the risen Lord now lives in those who believe in him: "It is no longer I who live, but Christ who lives in me" (2:20, RSV). "Christ in us" will mean living for Christ's sake a life for others. It may mean losing a job because we will not participate in the manufacture of nuclear weapons. It may mean rejecting or abandoning an attractive position in Boston or Washington to work with the poor in the third world. It may mean deciding to live in the scarred inner city rather than in the pleasant suburbs. It will certainly mean risking the disapproval of our friends, colleagues, and parishioners by clearly and persistently announcing the biblical word that God is on the side of the poor and that God calls us to be peacemakers. Because Christ lives in us, we have the spiritual energy to choose the difficult. We will be able to exhibit the same kind of love that Christ revealed in dying for us precisely because the God who raised our Lord Jesus now raises us to a new life for others.

The Christian view of death is my third illustration of how Jesus' resurrection radically shapes what Christians think. Over the ages, death has seemed to pose a terrifying threat. Modern secular people, of course, pretend otherwise. The secular philosopher Bertrand Russell assured us that there is no need to tremble at the idea that death ends personal existence forever. We die, rot, and that's it. Most people, of course, merely buy life insurance and try not to think about it. But what ultimate meaning does personal existence possess if it exists for a mere three score years or, perhaps by reason of modern medicine, four score years, and then passes into sheer nothingness?

The Marxist philosopher Ernst Bloch thought that the relative neglect of the problem of death in modern secular thought was due to the unconscious influence of inherited Christian views:

> Death (we do not know for how long) can only be suppressed so well because new life was once hidden behind it; that is, it was dreamed about and believed to be there. . . . The paltry confession to nothing (Nichts) would hardly be sufficient to keep the head high and to work as if there were no end. Rather clear signs indicate that earlier and richer forms of wishful dreams continue and give support in the subconscious. Through what remains from these ideals, the so-called modern man does not feel the chasm that unceasingly surrounds him and that certainly will engulf him at last. Through these remnants he saves, quite unawares, his sense of self-identity. Through them the impression arises that man is not perishing. . . . Thus in its ability to suppress the anxiety of all earlier times, apparently this quite shallow courage [of modern secular people] feasts on a borrowed credit card. It lives from earlier hopes and the support that they once had provided.[10]

Christians appreciate Bloch's exposé of secular shallowness in the face of the ultimate reality of death. But we insist that the ancient hope for life after death is not wishful dreaming but assured reality. Christians believe that death is not a terrifying passage into nothingness but rather a transition into a glorious eternity in the presence of the risen Lord Jesus. Why do Christians believe that? Because one person, Jesus of Nazareth, has already experienced death in all its fullness and returned from the dead to live forever. Christians believe that death is not a terrifying threat, because the tomb was empty, because the One with whom the disciples had lived appeared to them and assured them that he was alive forevermore. We await the risen Lord Jesus and therefore can declare with Paul, "'Death has been swallowed up in victory. Where, O death is your victory?'... Thanks be to God! He gives us the victory through our Lord Jesus Christ" (1 Corinthians 15:54-57, NIV).

With this view of death, the Christian can act courageously today. Life at any cost is not our motto; death for the King's cause is not disastrous. Paul said: "If we live, we live for the Lord; and if we die, we die for the Lord. . . . For this very reason, Christ died and returned to life so that he might be the Lord of both the dead and the living" (Romans 14:8-9, NIV). Because Christ is Lord of the living and the dead, we dare to face racists and militarists for the sake of our sisters and brothers; we dare to go as missionaries into dangerous situations; we dare to leave comfortable classrooms and secure homes to try to apply Jesus' call to peace and justice in the halls of government; we dare to join the poor in the swirling abyss of oppressive situations around the world.

Jesus' resurrection has transformed what Christians think and what Christians seek to do. In a few minutes, we will have the opportunity for a vigorous time of question and answer. I look forward to that. But before I end the lecture, I want to show how the kind of evangelical Christianity I am describing works out concretely in the tough issues of our time: our ravaged environment, our violence-torn inner cities, and our devastated families. And I am going to make a strong claim that I am sure many will want to challenge in the discussion. I am going to argue that biblical Christianity offers a better solution to these and other problems than the alternatives people are trying.

First a word on methodology. Whenever I seek to articulate my position on a contemporary issue, I try to bring together two things: (1) a carefully researched understanding of the full conceptual framework and ethical principles that the Bible teaches and (2) a thorough understanding of the full resources of modern thought (the social sciences, natural sciences, etc.). The Bible is my authority for faith and practice (for theology and ethics). But the Bible does not talk about whether we should build nuclear reactors or keep the comatose on life-support systems for years. To answer those questions, we have to combine biblical principles with sophisticated contemporary social and scientific analysis.

1. *Our environmental crisis.* The crisis is real and urgent. We must change not only our actions but our beliefs. Even secular people like prominent astrophysicist Carl Sagan are pleading with the religious community to get involved. But what religious ideas will truly help us?

Some people are turning to varieties of Eastern monism. New Age folk like the actress Shirley MacLaine say the solution is Eastern monism, which teaches that all is divine.

But notice a couple things. First of all, if monism is right and all is divine, then all is good, and you cannot even distinguish between good and evil. Furthermore, the ideal in Eastern monism is to escape this material world, turn within, and merge with the All. The material world is an illusion. The ideal is to merge with the Divine All in the way a drop of water falls into the ocean and disappears. The individual person loses all individual identity.

How does that worldview offer a solution to our environmental crisis? If the material world is an illusion, why worry about it?

Biblical faith is radically different. You and I and all the world around us are not divine. But we are very important. We are the creation of an all-powerful, all-loving Creator. We are finite but good. The material world is so good that the God of the universe, the Creator of the galaxies, became flesh on this little blue planet. The material world is so good that Jesus Christ rose bodily from death. The material world is so good that Jesus Christ promises to return to this earth and complete the victory over injustice, evil, and death itself.

Some environmentalists say persons are no more important than monkeys or moles or mushrooms, that to claim a special status for people is speciesism. But if that is true, then civilization collapses. They say we have no right to eat anything or use anything in the world around us. But redivinizing the material world is not the answer. In the film *Out of Africa*, the animists say they cannot build a dam because the water spirits live at the sea.

The biblical view is a carefully balanced view. Humans alone are created in the image of God, and we have the special task of being God's stewards over the rest of creation on this planet. The Genesis story that talks about this says persons are to "care for" God's garden. The word actually means to serve it.

The Bible also says that the nonhuman creation has independent worth and significance entirely apart from you and me. The heavens declare the glory of God. The sun, moon, and stars sing praises to their Creator. The Creator cares about every endangered species. So should we.

Christians have often neglected this full biblical teaching on the creation. And we have, along with Enlightenment naturalists, helped destroy the environment. For that, I repent. But I believe biblical faith offers a far better foundation for lovingly caring for this gorgeous creation than does Eastern monism or goddess worship.

2. *Our inner cities.* I lived in one of the most desperate parts of Philadelphia for seven years. The violence, drug abuse, unemployment, and family chaos are almost unbelievable. And the causes are complex: racism; global economic forces that moved jobs to third-world countries; wrong personal choices about drugs, sex, and alcohol.

How do we solve it? The government has been trying to do that for decades. We have spent hundreds of billions of dollars on well-intentioned programs to renovate housing, provide Head Start, improve the schools, and so on. A few things have helped. But the problems get worse and worse.

Biblical faith says we have missed half of the problem. For wholeness, people need both a good external environment and internal integrity grounded in a right relationship to God.

Let me tell you two stories. James Dennis is one of my special friends. For several years, we served together as elders in an inner-city church. Twenty years ago, James Dennis was an angry Black militant. He hated whites. A few years ago, he said that if he had met me back then, he might have killed me. Thank God, he met Jesus first!

Like so many inner-city young men with few decent job opportunities, James became an alcoholic. His marriage was in trouble, and he landed in prison for a serious crime. While there, someone shared the gospel with him, and he began to experience the transforming grace of Jesus Christ. When he left prison, our pastor walked beside him, supporting and discipling him, and James became an active member and then an elder in our church.

James Dennis is a radically different person today. He is still a proud African American who will not tolerate even the hint of white racism, but God erased his racial hatred and restored his family. He has a good job and owns his own home. Transforming grace has invaded his life.

Anybody who thinks that the best government programs on jobs, housing, and prison reform would have been enough to solve James Dennis's problems simply doesn't get it. He needed a personal relationship with Jesus Christ, which has transformed the core of his being, his values, inner convictions, and family life. At the same time, anybody who thinks that being born again, by itself, would have been enough to solve his problems doesn't get it either.

James Dennis can be as born again as you like, but if the inner-city school system offers his children a lousy education, if decent housing is unavailable, and if no jobs are to be found, he still has big problems.

Raleigh Washington is the African American pastor of Rock of Our Salvation Evangelical Free Church—an inner-city, interracial congregation on the West Side of Chicago. Intimately connected with the church is Circle Urban Ministries, a holistic community center led by Glen Kehrein, a white farm boy from Wisconsin. Circle has a medical clinic with seven full-time doctors, a legal clinic with two full-time lawyers, a low-income-housing program that has renovated millions of dollars of housing for the poor, and job-creation programs to build an economic base in the inner city. But the community center staff know that unless they offer more than excellent medical or legal help, they will never get to the heart of the problems and produce lasting change. So, when they sense a spiritual need, doctors and lawyers feel free to speak of Christ, or they encourage the person to arrange a visit with one of the chaplains who now works in both the community center and the church. Hundreds of people have come to personal faith in Christ. The result has been a rapidly growing inner-city congregation with more than three hundred members.

Rock/Circle is just one of hundreds of examples of committed Christian congregations daring to live and work in the midst of the agony of our inner cities to provide a holistic solution.

Of course, the government has a crucial role to play. There must be quality schools, decent housing and, above all, jobs that pay a living wage. But unless people are changed from the inside out, unless racism is overcome in our hearts, unless our families are restored, the best government programs will fail.

3. *Family and feminism.* Everybody knows that in general the American family is a disaster area. Social scientists regularly report the sad fact that children from homes where parents are divorced do more poorly in school, are more likely to get into crime, and so on. Furthermore, our society experiences incredible levels of rape, incest, and all kinds of sexual and physical violence against women.

The answer is not some kind of conservative religious patriarchy where the husband dominates the home, ruling wife and children as lord and master. In fact, that kind of patriarchy probably contributes to sexual abuse in the home.

But neither is the solution the kind of radical feminism that prefers lesbianism to marriage and places personal self-fulfillment above responsibility to children.

Biblical faith is just what we need. Jesus Christ, as we saw, was a feminist. He lived a radical challenge to the male chauvinists of his day, treating women as equals. The overarching principle that the apostle Paul spelled out for husbands and wives in Ephesians 5 is mutual submission. Jesus calls men and women to sexual purity and joyful lifelong marriage covenant.

Let me put it personally. My wife, Arbutus, and I have been married for thirty-two years. We believe in full mutuality in our marriage. We make our decisions together. We love sex, even at fifty-four, but we have never had sex with anyone else. There have been times in our marriage when we have hurt each other and struggled. We needed six months of marriage counseling once. But we were and are committed to each other for life, so we worked through those difficulties to a time of even greater joy and love. Our three children have never worried that we would get a divorce. We are both feminists—biblical feminists like Jesus, whom we love and worship.

I think the full biblical view of family, marriage, and the equality of women is what our aching homes need. You cannot have happy marriages if you screw around all through college and are never sure, even after marriage, if your partner will be faithful to you. Your marriage will not last if you see it as a limited contract that you will dissolve as soon as it does not feel good and fails to fulfill your immediate personal needs. The demand for instant gratification and self-centered individualism are central causes of the hell that rampages through our marriages.

There is a better way—the way that Jesus taught. It is possible—and in the long run full of greater joy and fulfillment—to reserve sex for marriage, to be faithful to your spouse. The full biblical view of family and feminism is just what this hurting society needs.

One final concluding point. Jesus teaches high standards. So, what happens when we fail? And we often do, as God knows— and as the media loves to report. Well, the cross of Jesus Christ is, I think, an astonishing answer. Christians believe that Jesus Christ took upon himself the punishment that our evil deeds deserve. So, our holy God forgives our terrible acts against others and God.

The awful evil that you and I do to neighbors poses a terrible problem. Let me be personal. There was a period in our marriage when Arbutus and I hurt each other rather deeply. We could have said, "Aw, shucks, it doesn't matter. It was nothing. Forget it." That would have been pure nonsense. It hurt like hell. Or we could have said, "That's it. I cannot forgive you." But then our relationship and the deep love we had shared for two decades would have ended.

Instead, we did on a microcosmic scale what God did at the cross. Arbutus looked at me and said, "What you did was very evil. But I love you. I accept the pain of the evil you did to me, and I forgive you. Let's walk on together." I did the same for her. It wasn't easy, and it didn't happen in a day, a month, or even a year. But the result has been renewed joy and wonderful happiness.

According to the Bible, sin is a terrible thing. It cannot be ignored. Hitlers and Stalins and wife beaters and liars and oppressors and rapists and racists all deserve punishment. So do guys who take advantage of women sexually at Colorado College.

But at the cross, God in Jesus Christ, who is very God, suffered the hell of a Roman crucifixion because the holy Creator combines justice and love in an awesome integration. God suffers the punishment you and I deserve so that evil deeds can be forgiven, so that broken people can be reconciled. You see, the only alternative to divine and human forgiveness is an ever-widening circle of broken relationships, hostility, and violence.

In conclusion, I don't pretend that evangelicals have always lived up to the high standards I have sketched. We have often failed to follow Jesus. But that is what we believe. And with the power of the risen Christ in our lives, that is how we seek to live.

Why would anybody want to be an evangelical? One, because biblical faith is true. And second, because it works. If you don't believe me, I challenge you to examine the evidence—openly without bias. And then I dare you to try it.

Notes

1. See https://news.gallup.com/poll/20242/another-look-evangelicals-america-today.aspx and https://news.gallup.com/poll/1690/religion.aspx.

2. Carl Sagan, *Cosmos* (New York: Random House, 2013).

3. Gary Habermas and Anthony Flew, *Did Jesus Rise from the Dead? The Resurrection Debate* (San Francisco: Harper, 1987), 3. For an extensive scholarly discussion of the evidence for Jesus' resurrection, see N. T. Wright, *The Resurrection of the Son of God* (Minneapolis: Fortress, 2003), and his more popular *Surprised by Hope* (New York: HarperOne, 2008).

4. Reginald H. Fuller, *The Formation of the Resurrection Narratives* (New York: Macmillan, 1971), 2.

5. Pinchas Lapide, *The Resurrection of Jesus: A Jewish Perspective* (Minneapolis: Augsburg, 1983), 16.

6. Lapide, 125.

7. Robert Grant, *Historical Introduction to the New Testament* (New York: Harper, 1963), 376.

8. Wolfhart Pannenberg, *Jesus: God and Man* (Philadelphia: Westminster, 1968), 100; italics in original.

9. C. F. D. Moule, ed., *Studies in Biblical Theology* 8 (London: SCM, 1968), 9.

10. Ernst Bloch, *Das Prinzip Hoffnung*, 2nd ed. (Frankfurt: Suhrkamp, 1959), 2:1360–61; quoted in Pannenberg, *Jesus*, 84.

CHAPTER 9

Needed: A Few More Scholars/ Popularizers/Activists

Personal Reflections on My Journey

A version of this piece was first presented as a paper at the Calvin College Conference "Christian Scholarship . . . for What?" (September 28, 2001). I later published an edited version in *Christian Scholar's Review* (vol. 36 [2007], 159–66). Today, twenty years later, I think that the need for some scholars who are also popularizers and activists is even greater than in 2001.

Church and society are often misled by people offering simplistic, one-sided answers to the big issues of their time. They pretend to know what they are talking about even though they lack the necessary expertise. Evangelicalism, especially, with its strong anti-intellectual strain, has often—whether one thinks of eschatology, science, family life, or politics—been badly served by popularizers and activists with simplistic ideas and superficial solutions. Nor will that change unless more people with good scholarly training become effective popularizers and successful activists.

I am a scholar who spent several years of my life completing a PhD at Yale to become a specialist on the sixteenth-century Reformation in Europe but ended up teaching only one course in my whole career in my area of academic specialization. I did publish two scholarly books and a few technical articles in the area of my dissertation. But when people come up and thank me for my book, I assume they mean *Rich Christians in an Age of Hunger*, not my scholarly book on the sixteenth-century reformer Andreas Bodenstein von Karlstadt.[1] For better or worse, I am best known as a popularizer. In fact, my problem, if it is a problem, runs even deeper. I have tried not only to combine popularizing with scholarly work but have also been an activist and organizer.

Frustrations and Danger

Trying to do what I have done, however, is inevitably problematic for several reasons. First, good popular writing almost inevitably requires an interdisciplinary understanding that no single scholar possesses. The general public has little interest in simply that aspect of world hunger, for example, discussed in technical detail with professional expertise by the professor of business or the professor of economic history or of small business development or of Christian ethics or Old Testament or New Testament—the list goes on and on. But all those specialties and more relate directly to the question: What is a faithful Christian response to world hunger today? The typical Christian layperson wants to read a coherent, reliable response to that broad question, not some specialized, technical paper that deals with one small aspect of the problem. Unfortunately, no scholar, however brilliant, is familiar with all those fields. Hence, every popularizing scholar knows they are doing what in a sense they have no business doing.

Second, because of the complexity just noted, there is never enough time to read even half of the relevant literature. Anybody who has done a PhD knows how to do exhaustive research and has strong inner inhibitions against starting to write before reading most of the relevant literature. For the interdisciplinary popularizer, that is not possible.

Third, popularization requires simplification. That is not to say that simplistic distortion is inevitable. But good popularizing demands that one set aside many complexities in order to offer a clear, coherent statement of the central issues. That easily frustrates the popularizer who is also a scholar—not to mention the scholarly critics who are not popularizers!

Fourth, the popularizer runs the danger of losing touch with his or her field of scholarly expertise. This is not inevitable. It depends on the relative amounts of time one puts into the two areas and also how closely connected one's scholarship and popular writing are. In my case, as a Reformation historian, there was little direct connection. In the early years after grad school, I managed to publish two scholarly books and a few articles on the Reformation. But ten years later, when asked to write an encyclopedia article on Karlstadt, it took only about ten minutes to conclude that I had neither the time nor the interest in spending the month or two of research needed to catch up on the scholarship enough to accept the invitation. I declined, with a twinge of regret, realizing that was the end of my work in an area to which I devoted at least five years of my life.

My activist, organizing work began in 1972. In late summer, I returned to the United States from several weeks of academic labor, finalizing the sixteenth-century Latin and German footnotes of my doctoral dissertation so that it could be published in the scholarly series Studies in Medieval and Reformation Thought, edited by Professor Heiko Oberman of Tübingen (and earlier, Harvard) University. In the huge pile of mail I encountered on my return, I discovered an appeal sent to evangelicals across the country to donate funds to support evangelical Republican Senator Mark Hatfield's reelection campaign. I made a small contribution and then soon felt moved to organize a small evangelical political effort, Evangelicals for McGovern, that resulted in a story in *Newsweek*. A follow-up letter to our donors led to a spring meeting at the first Calvin College Conference on Christian Faith and Politics. The meeting at Calvin led to the Thanksgiving 1973 Chicago Declaration of Evangelical Social Concern and the founding of Evangelicals for Social Action (ESA) in 1974, which I have led for all but one year since then. Even though I have had a full-time academic appointment for almost all of the years since 1968, I have invested vast amounts of time and energy in organizational and activist work on social issues.

During my career, I have tried to combine the roles of scholar, popularizer, and activist. In this essay, I first will describe five different "models" or approaches (three earlier efforts and then two more recent ones) in my attempt to combine scholarship, popularization, and activism. Especially in the last two, I can see an approach or model that may have applicability beyond my personal history.

Five "Models"

In early 1996 I opened a packed press conference at the National Press Club in Washington with a prayer and then a statement declaring that this was God's creation, and therefore evangelical Christians were concerned about endangered species. There were two reasons for the Washington journalists' interest and the flood of resulting news stories on national TV that night and scores of newspapers across the country in the next few days: first, a live cougar at the press conference, representing endangered species; and second, the fact that this dramatic public stand by ESA and the Evangelical Environmental Network (EEN) contradicted the widespread belief that all evangelical Christians were in the pocket of the new conservative Republican majority in Congress, which, in the view of many, was seeking to drastically weaken the Endangered Species Act.

It was my activist side that carried me into the environmental movement. I was generally concerned but had not written any popularizing, much less any scholarly, things on the topic when, in the early '90s, a caller from New York informed me that someone had told him that I was an evangelical who cared about the environment. Would I help gather evangelical leaders to a meeting in New York City? I agreed, and that led eventually to the very successful interreligious coalition called the National Religious Partnership for the Environment. EEN, which I put together in the early years with the help of people like Bob Seiple of World Vision and University of Wisconsin scholar Calvin DeWitt, became the evangelical partner along with the United States Catholic Conference, the National Council of Churches, and the Coalition on the Environment and Jewish Life.

With no scholarly preparation on the topic, I have relied on scholars like Cal DeWitt, Loren Wilkinson, and many others to try to make sure I get my facts straight. All my writing on the topic has been shorter popularizing pieces.

The second effort focused on the issue of Jesus' resurrection. In this case, I have combined scholarly and popularizing articles. My interest goes back to a period of vigorous intellectual doubt during my second year of college and then the appointment of evangelical historian John Warwick Montgomery as the new chairman of the history department for my junior and senior years as an undergraduate history major at Waterloo College in Canada. I embraced Montgomery's passion for scholarship and apologetics based on a historical argument for Jesus' resurrection. A couple of years later when I was a leader of the InterVarsity-related Yale Graduate Fellowship and a doctoral student in history, it was almost inevitable that I would lecture to the group on the historical evidence for Jesus' resurrection.

That lecture—which I still give in much revised form—has gone through a lot of permutations and been published in at least a dozen different forms. My thinking has also benefited from considerable further study and writing. My sense of call at the time I first gave this lecture as a graduate student was to be a good Renaissance-Reformation scholar teaching in a secular university where I would offer a low-key intellectual apologetic for historic Christianity. To deepen both my biblical and theological preparation for that task and to experience more of the full force of the modern challenge to orthodox Christianity, I decided to interrupt my doctoral program in history after I completed my comprehensive exams and spend three years at Yale Divinity School. While there, I wrote a long paper on 1 Corinthians 15 for a class with New Testament professor Nils Dahl, which eventually appeared as two separate articles in two scholarly New Testament journals—*New Testament Studies* and *Novum Testamentum*. A somewhat technical article on historical methodology published in the *Scottish Journal of Theology* in 1972 added depth to my analysis. It also led to a fellowship in 1976 and many months of study preparing to write a scholarly book on historical methodology and the miraculous (which was never completed).

The third illustration—*Rich Christians in an Age of Hunger* and related publications and organizing efforts—is much more widely known than the previous two. With sales of more than five hundred thousand copies in seven languages, *Rich Christians* is my most successful effort at popularization. Had I known what I now do, I would have made quite different choices as a student to prepare for writing about world hunger and economic justice. I have only taken one—and that an introductory undergraduate—course in economics in my life. I did not take any courses in social ethics in my three years at Yale Divinity School in the '60s! I was simply not prepared either in economics or social ethics to write *Rich Christians*. Probably my best scholarly preparation for *Rich Christians* came from a number of courses in biblical studies at Yale Divinity School, and it may be significant that the best part of *Rich Christians*, and the part that has changed the least in the five revisions, is part 2 on a biblical perspective.

The whole project started quite unintentionally as a sermon on world hunger for a tiny church in 1967. As I completed my sermon that Saturday afternoon, I felt that I should add some practical application to the two sections on the facts about world hunger and a biblical framework. The idea of a graduated tithe came to me, so I included it in the sermon, and my wife, Arbutus, and I began to practice it. A few years later, InterVarsity Christian Fellowship's *His* magazine published a short article titled "The Graduated Tithe." Then InterVarsity Press gave me a contract to do a short book with the same name. But it grew like Topsy as I wrote it, and for almost the only time in my career as an author, the publisher never argued even once with the title I suggested: *Rich Christians in an Age of Hunger*.

Knowing my lack of preparation in economics, I asked a number of friends who were economists to read the early drafts. I did not always take their advice, but they certainly helped me avoid some mistakes. A Calvin grad and doctoral student in economics, Roland Hoksbergen, greatly improved the economic analysis in the second edition in 1984. A couple years later, I joined Vinay Samuel in organizing a nine-year process called the Oxford Conference on Christian Faith and Economics, which brought together a wonderfully diverse circle of scholars (economists, business professors, biblical scholars, and ethicists) as well as business leaders and activists from around the world. That, too, deepened my scholarly analysis and strengthened subsequent editions.

Activism and organizing have also been a central part of my work in this third area: organizing international conferences on simple lifestyle and development; leading more than two decades of activity in ESA on the topic; founding and coediting the semi-popular, semi-scholarly international journal *Transformation*; giving hundreds of speeches and writing dozens of short articles on world hunger; and, after I wrote the first edition, seeing poverty firsthand in my travels in Africa, Asia, and Latin America.

A fourth experience, which started about 1995, has more of the right components for combining scholarship, popularization, and activism than any earlier efforts. Evangelicals for Social Action received a substantial grant to work on the question "If the United States truly wanted to reduce domestic poverty dramatically, what would be the full range of things that government and other sectors in society would need to do simultaneously?" From the beginning, we set up the two-year-plus process as an interdisciplinary scholarly effort. We sought out the best evangelical scholars in all of the major areas that we knew needed simultaneous attention because they were all interlocked. Several scholars agreed to write foundational pieces dealing with underlying philosophical, and biblical-theological issues to provide a conceptual framework. Others worked on specific aspects, including health care, education, and income.

All the authors met together at regular intervals to discuss one another's developing drafts, argue about competing interpretations, and suggest improvements. Initially, we planned simply to publish this collection of scholarly essays (which Baker Publishing Group did in 1999, in a book called *Toward a Just and Caring Society: Christian Responses to Poverty in America*, edited by David Gushee).

Partway through the process, however, it dawned on me that in addition to coauthoring one of the chapters of the scholarly volume, I should consider writing a shorter, more popular book drawing on the careful chapters being written for the scholarly volume. Everyone seemed to agree, so I set to work carefully rereading all the scholars' chapters, but also delving on my own into some of the most significant scholarship and data on the issues that I chose to highlight. I benefited enormously from the work done by the contributors to the scholarly volume. Several of them also agreed to read my first draft, and virtually everyone reviewed any section related to their special expertise. *Just*

Generosity: A New Vision for Overcoming Poverty in America was the result. Since the book had the good fortune of appearing just as American society was taking a vigorous new look at the role of faith-based programs, I was able, thanks in part to ESA and its members, to use the results of this process in a variety of activist ways, including several editorials in major newspapers, lobbying, speaking, short popular articles, and consulting in Washington.

I think this is a promising model for Christian scholars who seek to contribute to the public policy debate. The broad interdisciplinary approach of this process enabled us to look, if not at the whole picture, then at least at a large part of it, and develop a comprehensive response to poverty based on solid scholarship. Few people, however, read collections of scholarly essays by a group of different scholars, and publishers are reluctant to publish them. They are simply too technical and often lack a tightly integrated argument. *Just Generosity* tried to state the comprehensive vision in a much briefer, more readable, integrated argument.[2] If I had been a more powerful writer and if ESA had had more organizing capacity, the results could have been much greater. This model—combining scholarship, popularization, and activism—could be used effectively on a wide range of public policy issues.

The last, and most recent, approach also combines scholarship, popularizing, and activism as I have dealt with the interrelationship between evangelism and social action in faith-based ministries. In this case, however, it was a brilliant graduate assistant, rather than academic colleagues, who provided the interdisciplinary help.

Sometime in 1994 I had requested a grant from the Lilly Endowment to study what difference it made when congregations running social ministries also included a strong evangelistic component. They were interested but wanted the proposal to interact in more detail with the considerable body of research on congregations that they had supported over several decades. I simply did not have the time immediately to study all of that literature carefully. So, I asked Heidi Rolland, a very bright Wheaton sociology graduate who was then studying with me at Eastern Baptist Theological Seminary, to do an independent study with me, analyze that literature, and help refine the grant proposal. When we received the grant, she became the associate director of what became a five-year project studying the diverse ways that evangelism and social ministry interacted in fifteen different congregations.

In early 2002, Baker published the popular book *Congregations That Make a Difference*, drawing on this research but aimed at local congregational leaders, written by Heidi, Phil Olson, and me. Heidi and I also completed a scholarly volume, *Saving Souls, Serving Society: Understanding the Faith Factor in Church-Based Social Ministry*, published by Oxford University Press in 2005, reporting on the same research for the scholarly and public policy communities.

In this process, Heidi and I also drew on the scholarly expertise of others in several ways. Grant funds enabled us to use scholarly consultants. As I have in most of my interdisciplinary work, we also asked friends who are specialists in specific areas to review early drafts.

This research had the good fortune of occurring at the same time that scholars like John Dilulio, the secular media, public policy elites, and the political world discovered that faith-based organizations were sometimes highly successful in desperately broken communities where almost everything else had failed. We were unusually well prepared to participate in the national debate about charitable choice and faith-based organizations when it hit the front pages of our newspapers in 2000 and 2001. As a result, Heidi and I have given papers and participated in panels and study projects in Washington and elsewhere at a level beyond anything I had done in the past. We have published shorter articles based on this research in everything from the *Brookings Review* (and a Brookings book edited by John Dilulio and E. J. Dionne), to *Christianity Today*, to several major newspapers.

This model, combining scholarship, popularizing, and activism, worked well because of (1) major foundation grants; (2) a gifted graduate student with training in a crucial discipline (sociology) where I had no expertise; (3) ESA's long track record on holistic ministry; (4) good connections to important public policy conversations through my friendship with John Dilulio; and (5) the good fortune to be completing significant research on an issue just as it became one of the hottest topics in national political debate.

What generalizations and conclusions do I draw from this brief sketch of my personal pilgrimage in combining scholarship, popularizing, and activism?

First, as much as possible, I think it is desirable to do research and write a scholarly piece on a topic before publishing a popular piece. (I formulated that as a personal guideline some years ago, but I have not been able, or at least have not taken the time, to do it consistently.)

Second, since popularizing usually requires interdisciplinary knowledge, I have found it very helpful to develop friendships with experts in the relevant fields. I try to listen carefully to their advice without being intimidated by them.

Third, I have sought to find expert, interdisciplinary help whenever I could, whether via grants, a graduate assistant, a collaborative scholarly project, or at least friends who are experts in other disciplines.

Fourth, I have tried to accept the fact that I cannot read all the relevant literature, but I study carefully a short selection of the best publications and make sure I read authors from all the major competing approaches to the topic.

Fifth, I seek to make modest claims, acknowledge my weaknesses, and remain ready to modify my position when further data warrants that.

Finally, a few conclusions. First, good popularizing requires special skills, an ability to develop a broad synoptic vision, an instinct for quickly discerning the most crucial issues, a personality and mind that enjoy moving quickly from one issue to another, and the ability to write clearly and powerfully.

Second, one must recognize that the kinds of choices I have made have consequences. While there are a few exceptions, like Martin Marty, most people cannot attempt the level of popularizing and activism I have sought and also become a widely recognized scholar.

Third, I would discourage anyone from trying to do what I have done unless you feel called and friends confirm that you have the necessary gifts and thereby confirm that call. Not many people should do it! I do not mean for a moment to urge most scholars to abandon a life of extended, focused scholarly research in their specific area of professional expertise. What I have tried is not for everyone.

Finally, some scholars must do it. Plato said that if the wise disdain the task of politics, then they must suffer being governed by fools. Somebody will write popularizing books for "the average person." If those with scholarly training will not do it, they should not complain when those with little expertise do it badly, embarrassing the church and misleading laypeople with one-sided, simplistic nonsense.

I hope that a few in each generation of Christian scholars will pray for the gifts, develop the skills, and pay the price of becoming far better popularizers and more effective activists than I have managed to be.

Notes

1. Ronald J. Sider, *Rich Christians in an Age of Hunger: Moving from Affluence to Generosity*, 6th ed. (Nashville: W Publishing Group, 2015); Sider, *Andreas Bodenstein von Karlstadt: The Development of His Thought, 1517–1525* (Leiden: E. J. Brill, 1974).

2. Somewhat similar to the approach in this fourth "model" is the process that led to the National Association of Evangelicals' declaration "For the Health of the Nation: An Evangelical Call to Civic Responsibility," unanimously adopted by the NAE board in October 2004. Diane Knippers and I cochaired a several-year process that brought together a broad range of evangelical scholars with expertise in a variety of areas needed to develop the beginnings of an evangelical political philosophy. In the course of several meetings, we reviewed and refined each other's essays, which Baker published in 2005 in *Toward an Evangelical Public Policy: Political Strategies for the Health of the Nation* (coedited by Diane Knippers and me). The draft of the brief, popular document "For the Health of the Nation" emerged out of the more scholarly essays. Again, the book appeared at an unusually propitious moment—soon after the 2004 elections when the secular media focused enormous attention on the political views of evangelical voters. The result was numerous stories in major national newspapers.

CHAPTER 10

Open Letter to
Young Evangelicals

At the age of seventy-two, I felt the urge to write an open letter to evangelical Christians who were thirty-five to forty-five years younger than me. When *Relevant* magazine published it in their March–April 2011 issue under the title "An Open Letter to This Generation," they received a huge response. At eighty-one years of age, I continue to consider it a precious gift when much younger people are open to dialogue. I try hard to listen carefully and also to share my best insight.

Just writing that title feels a bit strange. For a long time, people called me a "young evangelical." Actually, the adjectives were sometimes less gracious: "radical" or "leftist" or "Marxist." (My response to the label "Marxist" was simple: "I'm a Mennonite farm boy, for Pete's sake. Have you ever met a Mennonite farmer who wants the government to own his land?") So I used to be a "radical young evangelical." But I was born in 1939, so, however reluctantly, I have long since had to abandon the label "young." Hence this open letter to a generation of truly young evangelicals, many of whom are forty years younger than I am.

I have no desire to lecture you or "set you straight." I have enormous appreciation for this generation of young evangelicals. Forty years ago, when some of my young evangelical friends and I started talking about social justice, racial justice, God's special concern for the poor, and holistic mission that combined evangelism and social action, we were considered radical.

Much is different today. Not all older evangelicals "get it," but large numbers of you younger evangelicals certainly do. A special concern for the poor and oppressed is part of your DNA. Caring for creation and transcending racial prejudice are simply who you are. You cannot imagine an evangelism that only cares about people's "souls." You just assume, without any need for argument, that biblical Christians should love the whole person the way Jesus did, offering both spiritual and material transformation. You want to engage the whole culture—art, music, literature, politics—rather than withdraw into some isolated ghetto. For all of this and much more, I shout, "Hallelujah!"

But there are four areas where I would love to have a dialogue. I have four questions that I would like to ask you to ponder. Do you care as much about inviting non-Christians to embrace Christ as Savior and Lord as you do about social justice? As you understand, thanks in part to postmodernism, that every person's thinking is limited by his or her specific location in space and time, are you in danger of abandoning the whole idea of moral and intellectual truth? Will you do a better job than my generation of keeping your marriage vows? As you rightly seek to respect the dignity and rights of gay and lesbian folk, have you considered carefully the church's millennia-long teaching on homosexuality?

I won't lecture you on these topics. Every generation of Christians must seek again to discern what biblical revelation means for their own time and place. All I ask is that you do that in dialogue with the whole church—the church of previous centuries, the worldwide church today, and yes, those of us who are now "older evangelicals." We will pray fervently for you as you do that and be most grateful when you seek us out for dialogue.

Let me explain my four questions.

First, is there any danger that your passion for social justice will lead to neglecting evangelism? I vigorously affirm your commitment to justice for the poor and your rejection of an evangelism that focuses only on the "soul" and neglects people's material needs. I have spent much of my life arguing on biblical grounds for precisely these concerns. But I have also watched some evangelical "social activists" lose their concern for evangelism.

Evangelism and social action should be inseparable. They are two sides of the same coin, but they are not identical. Working for economic development in poor communities or working for structural change to end systemic oppression is not the same thing as inviting persons who do not now confess Christ to embrace him as Lord and Savior. If we only do social action and never say we do it because of Christ, our good deeds point only to ourselves and make us look good. The Bible clearly teaches that humans are both material and spiritual beings. Both the Scriptures and human experience show that sin is personal and social. Social brokenness (including poverty) results from both wrong personal choices and unjust structures. If we work at only half the problem, we produce only half a solution. People need both personal faith in Christ, which transforms their values and very personality, and also material, structural transformation that brings new socioeconomic opportunities. That is why holistic evangelical community development programs that truly combine evangelism and social action (think of John Perkins and the Christian Community Development Association) work better now in this life.

But persons are made for far more than a good life here on earth for sixty or one hundred years. Every person is invited to live forever with the living God. Jesus died so that whoever believes in him may have both a better life now and life eternal.

Two other biblical truths are crucial. Jesus is the only way to salvation, and those who continue to reject Christ depart eternally from the living God. I know that my generation has sometimes said these things in harsh, insensitive ways. Too often we have failed to say with the Bible that God does not want anyone to perish (2 Peter 3:9).

But if the Bible is our norm, we dare not neglect its teaching that people are lost without Christ (Ephesians 2:12; 1 Thessalonians 1:9). Jesus (surely the most amazing Teacher of love the world has ever known) says more about eternal separation from the living God than anyone else in the Bible (e.g., Matthew 13:41-42, 49-50; 18:8; 25:41). Surely if Jesus is true God as well as true man, we cannot act as if he did not know what he was talking about.

Instead, we should embrace his claim that he is the way, the truth and the life. "No one comes to the Father except through me," Jesus said (John 14:6, NIV). For as Peter said at Pentecost, there is no other name under heaven by which we can be saved (Acts 4:12).

Of course, there are tough questions, for instance, about things like those who have never heard the gospel or about eternal punishment. (I wrestle with those in the chapter on evangelism in my *Good News and Good Works: A Theology for the Whole Gospel.*) But for most of church history, Christians have believed and taught the biblical affirmation that apart from Christ, people are eternally lost. Those parts of the modern church that have abandoned these truths have declined disastrously.

So, gently but clearly, I ask you to wrestle with the question, Do you care as much about lovingly inviting non-Christians to embrace the Savior as you do about social justice? Is there any danger that this generation of evangelical social activists will repeat the one-sidedness of the old social gospel and neglect evangelism? Will this generation of young evangelicals spend as much time, money, and effort praying and strategizing about how to winsomely invite non-Christians to come to Christ as you do working for social justice?

My second question is about truth. You have rightly learned from postmodernism that every person's ideas and beliefs are significantly shaped by their specific location in space and time. But do you still believe that there is moral and intellectual truth?

You are certainly correct to point out that Christians over the centuries, including this generation of older evangelicals, have been perversely shaped in their thinking by surrounding society. Augustine said dreadful things about sexuality, and Luther penned terrible comments about Jews. In my lifetime, too many older evangelicals were blatantly racist and homophobic. They largely ignored the hundreds of biblical texts about God's amazing concern for justice for the poor and marginalized. One older evangelical friend of mine told me thirty-five years ago that he had gone to evangelical Bible conferences for sixty years and never once heard a sermon on justice!

Far too often, older evangelicals have made absolute claims about their theological affirmations. We failed to see clearly that every human theological system contains human misunderstanding that comes from the fact that every theologian is a finite, imperfect, still painfully sinful person. Young evangelicals have learned that we must be far humbler in our theological claims.

But does that mean that truth does not exist? Sophisticated postmodernist thinkers say yes. They say all "truth" is simply a human construct produced by different groups of people to promote their self-interest. At the popular level, relativism reigns. Whatever I feel is right for me is "my truth." It is outrageous intolerance to tell someone else that they are wrong.

But finally, that kind of relativism—whether the sophisticated or the popular variety—does not work. If truth does not exist, science and civilization collapse. If, as Nietzsche claimed, no moral truth exists, then society is simply a vicious power struggle where the most powerful trample the rest. As the famous atheist philosopher Bertrand Russell said, those who have the best poison gas will have the ethics of the future. One of the best Christian antidotes to this kind of modern relativism is Pope John Paul II's great 1993 encyclical *The Splendor of Truth*.

The fact that my (and every other human's) understanding of truth, justice, and morality is dreadfully imperfect does not mean that intellectual and moral truth do not exist. God is truth. Christ is the truth. The Bible is God's revealed truth even though my understanding of it is very inadequate. That God is Father, Son, and Holy Spirit; that Jesus is true God and true man; that Jesus rose bodily form the dead; that Jesus' life, death, and resurrection are the only way to salvation for everyone—these are *unchanging truths* that will always be essential for every generation of Christians, even though we finite human beings never fully understand them. Not everything must change!

Contemporary culture confuses relativism and tolerance. In so many circles, it is considered intolerable to say that someone else's behavior and beliefs are wrong. But I can and should respect other people and defend their freedom to say and do things I consider wrong without abandoning my assertion that some actions are moral and others are immoral. We must vigorously reject society's equation of tolerance with relativism.

My prayer for this generation of young evangelicals is that you learn from postmodernists the many complex ways that our ideas and beliefs are shaped by our social setting without abandoning the historic Christian affirmation that moral and intellectual truth exists because it is grounded in God.

Third, a question about marriage. Will you young evangelicals be more faithful in keeping your marriage vows than my generation?

I weep over the pain and agony that so many of you have experienced in your homes. Through no choice of your own, you have had to suffer the anguish of broken families. So many of you could not enjoy the security of knowing that Mom and Dad would be faithful to each other for life. It saddens me to realize that some of you even fear to marry because of the anguish you have experienced due to your parents' broken marriages. That your evangelical parents got divorced at the same rate as the rest of society is one of the most blatant markers of Christian disobedience today.

The widespread agony in so many evangelical homes is a striking contrast to the joy of good Christian marriages. God's best gift to me, after his Son, is my wife, Arbutus, with whom I expect to celebrate our fiftieth wedding anniversary this August. Of course, we had troubled times. At the worst time, we needed the gifts of a wonderful Christian marriage counselor for six months. But the ongoing joy of a wife and husband growing together in mutual submission over many decades is an amazing gift of our Creator. And yes, even at seventy-one years of age, sex is still a delight.

The older I grow, the more certain I am that the Creator's design for sex and marriage truly works better than the alternatives. For a couple of years before our marriage, I carried a note in my wallet that promised God and myself I would wait until marriage to have sex. At the hardest times in our marriage, when I was severely tempted to commit adultery, God's holy commands protected me. Working through our painful struggles rather than running away from them has led to decades of happiness.

I want to plead with young evangelicals. Please resolve now to keep your promise to your spouse and children. Please live out a wonderful model of joyful, mutually submissive marriage that blesses your children with security and goodness and attracts non-Christians to the Savior. Forgiving each other for failures, working through the inevitable problems, and growing together for a lifetime are better for your children, better for the church, and better for society.

That is also the way to more lasting joy for you! One related question for you to ponder if you are not married is this: Can you look into the face of Christ and say, "Lord, I believe with all my heart that the way I am relating physically in my dating is pleasing to you"? If you cannot do that, are you willing to ask Christ to help you change your behavior so that it truly pleases the Lord? If you are not willing to behave now sexually in a way that is biblically obedient, why do you think you will later keep your marriage vows and spare your children the agony you have endured?

My young friends, the Creator's way really works much better than today's sexual promiscuity. I believe with all my heart that your generation of evangelicals can, in the power of the risen Lord, keep your marriage vows, experience joyous marriages, and thereby live winsome models of marital fidelity and happiness. I beg you, make that your goal, and then by God's grace do what it takes to reach it.

Finally, a question about the complex issue of homosexuality. Are young evangelicals quickly abandoning what older evangelicals believe on this issue without carefully examining biblical teaching and the near unanimous history of the church over almost two thousand years?

God knows, the older generation of evangelicals has dealt with this issue almost as poorly as possible. Many of us were homophobic. We tolerated gay bashers. We were largely silent when bigots in the society battered or even killed gay folk. We did not deal sensitively and lovingly with young people in our churches struggling with their sexual orientation. Instead of taking the lead in ministering to people with AIDS, some of our leaders even opposed government funding for research to discover medicine to help those with AIDS. At times we even had the gall to blame gay folk for the collapse of marriage in our society, ignoring the obvious fact that 95 percent of the people in this society are heterosexual. The primary reason for the collapse of marriage is the fact that the vast heterosexual majority (including evangelical Christians) have not kept their marriage vows.

I understand why you are less than enthusiastic about listening to older evangelicals on this issue. But is that an adequate reason for failing to wrestle carefully with the biblical material and the long teaching of the church over the centuries?

I don't have space here to discuss the details of biblical interpretation on this issue except to note that the primary biblical case against homosexual practice is not the few explicit biblical texts but rather the fact that in dozens of places the Bible talks about the goodness of sexual intercourse, and always the context is a marriage relationship between a man and a woman. There are many excellent books on the biblical material, including Duke New Testament professor Richard Hays's chapter 16 in *The Moral Vision of the New Testament* and Stanley J. Grenz's *Welcoming but Not Affirming*. See also my chapter 5 in *The Future of Our Faith*, edited with Ben Lowe.

One other fact complicates your task. The dominant media in secular culture are overwhelmingly committed to teaching everyone that the historic Christian teaching on sexuality is wrong and that heterosexual and homosexual (or bisexual) practice are equally valid personal choices. Hollywood, TV, intellectual elites, and major newspapers are all dreadfully biased. I pray that you will let the Bible and the church, rather than secular culture guide your thinking on this issue.

And please do not be misled by the theologically confused argument that since we are all sinners (which is true), therefore the church cannot say homosexual practice is sin. Just because every Christian continues to fail God in some ways does not mean we should abandon biblical norms and stop speaking of sin. Rather, we should reaffirm God's standards in every area of life, and then walk with each other to help each other become more and more conformed to the image of Christ.

Younger evangelicals are listening more carefully to Christian history, especially the writers of the first few centuries. Surely, therefore, you will thoughtfully weigh the fact that for almost two thousand years, Christians have taught overwhelmingly that God's will for sexual intercourse is within the marriage of a man and a woman.

Also important is careful listening to the Christians in the Global South, where a large majority of Christians now live. Here, too, young evangelicals are well ahead of my generation in overcoming the condescending, even racist attitudes of many white European/North American Christians. Therefore, I'm sure you will want to attach great significance to the fact that overwhelmingly, Christians in the South believe that homosexual practice is not God's will. (One of the more striking recent examples of white, "Western" arrogance is the way that relatively small Anglican/Episcopal churches in the West have refused to submit to the views of the vast majority of Anglicans worldwide who in fact reside in the Global South.) My prayers go with you as you dialogue with your sisters and brothers in the South on this and all issues.

Young evangelicals could embrace the church's historic teaching without repeating my generation's mistakes. Andrew Marin gives us just one example of how you can rightly have gay friends and seek to understand them. You can oppose gay bashing, insist on proper civil rights for gay Americans, and help the church take the lead in ministering to people with AIDS. You can and should insist that homosexual sin is no worse than other sins like adultery or racism or covetousness. You can and should insist that it is safe and acceptable for Christians to publicly acknowledge a gay orientation (orientation and practice are quite different issues) and seek the support of their Christian community for living celibate lives (such persons should be eligible for any office in the church). In short, young evangelicals could develop a radically different (and far more Christian!) approach to homosexual persons without abandoning the historic Christian position.

There you have my four questions. Thanks, young friends, for listening to someone who is thirty (or fifty!) years older than you are. On all these issues and many more, you will have to find your own way. Above all, remain unconditionally committed to Christ and uncompromisingly faithful to biblical revelation. I will pray for you as you seek to apply biblical faith to your complex world. And also, if you are willing, I'll be glad to continue the dialogue for a decade or three if the Lord continues to extend the gift of life.

CHAPTER 11

White Evangelicals, Racism, and Economic Justice

I gave this address in Memphis, Tennessee, on September 30, 2017, at a conference cosponsored by the Memphis Civil Rights Museum and the Memphis Center for Urban Theological Studies. Tragically, the problem of white evangelical racism has grown clearer since that time. The vast majority of white evangelicals has continued to support former president Donald Trump in spite of his continuing blatant racist actions and appeals. Now, after Donald Trump's election defeat in 2020, one of the biggest tasks for white evangelicals will be to wrestle honestly with their racism.

I stand before you as a white evangelical Christian. And that means bringing with me the tragic, sinful baggage that the label "evangelical" carries.

I confess that white evangelical racism is not just a recent phenomenon of the last two years—although the fact that 81 percent of white evangelicals voted for a man who clearly appealed to white racists is the most recent manifestation of that long, sad history. Thank God for those white evangelicals active in the 1830s, 1840s, and 1850s who opposed slavery. But other prominent white evangelical leaders at the same time defended slavery. And it was not just Southern evangelicals who defended slavery. White evangelicals also played a major role in the reversal of the progress made right after the end of the Civil War. When Dr. Martin Luther King Jr. marched for justice, white evangelicals, with a few exceptions, were at best silent and often critical. As one acknowledges this centuries-long sinful failure of white evangelicals, one can only weep, repent, and ask for forgiveness.

I understand why, given this history, the Black church has no interest in embracing the label "evangelical." In reality, I think, the African American church is closer to white evangelicals than to any other part of the American church in both piety and theology. The African American church, which uses labels like "Bible-believing," actually affirms many of the same basic theological commitments as do white evangelicals: Jesus is true God and true man. Jesus' life and death are the only way to salvation for all people. Jesus rose bodily from the dead on Easter morning. People need to come to a personal relationship with Jesus Christ so that their sins are forgiven and the Holy Spirit can transform them into renewed persons who live like Jesus. Black Bible-believing Christians and white evangelicals share those wonderful beliefs. But I clearly understand why, given the history of white evangelical racism, the Black church does not use the label "evangelical," with which I have been identified for almost all my life.

Personally, as a Bible-believing Christian (yes, one using the label "evangelical"), I have tried to work against white racism: in my speaking and writing; in living for many decades in a majority African American community in Philadelphia; in rejoicing in a Black son-in-law and a beautiful ten-year-old African American granddaughter. If you do not believe me that she is the most beautiful ten-year-old lady in the world, come after my speech and I'll show you her picture, which pops up every time I open my cell phone.

Way back in 1968, my wife and I lived in an apartment rented from an African American couple. We sat with them the evening Dr. King was murdered.

One of the most important privileges of my life was to chair the committee of Christian Churches Together in the USA that released the first response by a broad group of Christian leaders to Dr. King's "Letter from Birmingham Jail."[1] Christian Churches Together is a broad ecumenical movement in the US that brings together five major Christian families: Catholics, historic Protestant denominations, African American denominations, Orthodox denominations, and evangelical/Pentecostal denominations. As we wrestled with the issue of racism in a couple of our annual meetings, we realized that no substantial group of Christian leaders had ever responded to Dr. King's historic letter. So, we decided to do a response, and we issued it in Birmingham on April 16, 2013, on the fiftieth anniversary of Dr. King's historic letter.[2]

I want to mention several things from our response to Dr. King's "Letter from Birmingham Jail" because I think they help focus on what we need to do today. In our response to Dr. King, we noted several areas where we felt especially challenged by his original letter.

First, we felt deeply challenged by Dr. King's emphasis on our essential interdependence. "Injustice anywhere," he said, "is a threat to justice everywhere. We are caught in an inescapable network of mutuality."[3]

Second, we felt challenged by Dr. King's call to deal not just with the symptoms of injustice but also with the underlying causes.[4] Study after study has shown that although many white evangelicals declare their opposition to racism, they fail to understand the structural foundations of racial injustice. Structural factors have contributed to things like a Black unemployment rate double that of the white unemployment rate, and the fact that many largely white suburban schools offer higher-quality education than many largely African American or Hispanic inner-city schools.

Third, we felt challenged by Dr. King's call to be extremists for love, justice, and peace, which was also Jesus' call.[5] Following

Jesus means daring to speak boldly against injustice even when that makes us unpopular. It means daring to say that the people in Black Lives Matter are right that young African American men get shot by police more often than others and that this injustice must end now.

Fourth, we felt challenged to be more engaged in nonviolent direct action. In the fifty years since Dr. King's death, his nonviolent methods have been proven successful again and again in ways that probably would surprise even Dr. King. More than a million peaceful marchers succeeded in 1986 in overthrowing President Ferdinand Marcos, the decades-long vicious dictator of the Philippines. In 1989, Solidarity, the nonviolent movement of Polish citizens, defied and defeated Poland's powerful Communist dictatorship. In 2003 an amazing nonviolent movement of Liberian women defeated Charles Taylor, the country's brutal dictator, and led to democratic elections. If Dr. King were here today, I am sure he would lament the fact that in spite of more and more examples of nonviolent campaigns overthrowing dictators and promoting justice, our churches and governments invest almost no money for engaging in nonviolent campaigns. What would happen if the churches invested a few tens of millions of dollars in studying previous successful nonviolent campaigns and training thousands of people to prepare to engage in new nonviolent campaigns? What would happen if our government spent one-tenth as much in preparing for nonviolent promotion of peace and justice as it spends on military preparations?

Fifth, we felt challenged by Dr. King's call to be a thermostat that changes the temperature rather than just a thermometer that simply reflects the temperature.[6] So much of the church remains silent in the face of ongoing injustice. Only a few white evangelicals boldly condemned the public racism in our political life in the last two years, and some of those who did received vigorous criticism. So many white Christians fail to condemn the racial

179

inequality between the largely white suburban schools and largely nonwhite inner-city schools. If we are to stop being mere thermometers that silently acquiesce to this present, blatant, unjust inequality in our schools and want to become thermostats that bring genuine change, then white Christians will have to risk offending our neighbors and help lead the struggle for quality schools for everyone.

The issue of poverty in America today reflects many of the areas where the response to Dr. King's "Letter from Birmingham Jail" indicated important challenges. So I want to direct the rest of my comments to the topic of poverty. I think that is especially important since in the last years of his life, Dr. King was increasingly focused on poverty, especially with the Poor People's Campaign. And as we know, he was murdered here in Memphis, where he had come to support the garbage workers' demand for a just wage.

The data is clear—and points to glaring injustice. Today African Americans on average are at least twice as likely to be poor or unemployed as whites. In 2015 the unemployment rate for whites was 4.5 percent and for African Americans 10.3 percent. In terms of median net worth, white households are about thirteen times as wealthy as Black households—a gap that is actually wider today than in 1983. At every level of education, African Americans earn significantly less than whites. In fact, as a recent piece in *Forbes* magazine (September 21, 2016) reported, the difference in the average hourly real wage earned by white and Black Americans is actually greater today than in 1979.

I do not need to go on citing statistics to show that serious economic injustice related to racism continues in this country. And it is obvious that many white Americans either do not know about this injustice or do not care about it.

What can be done? For much of my life, I have lectured and written about poverty and economic injustice both here and abroad. In my experience, I have found that one of the best ways to help Christians who are not poor become involved in working for justice is to help them see what the Bible tells us about God's concern for economic justice. Combining biblical teaching with concrete suggestions about workable solutions helps us make progress. So, for the rest of this presentation, I want to remind us about a couple of key biblical teachings and then suggest some ways forward.

Two biblical themes are especially important: first, the Bible tells us that God is on the side of the poor; and second, sin is both personal and social or structural.

First, God and the poor. The Bible tells us in several ways that God acts in history to lift up the poor and oppressed. I like very much the way James Cone put this decades ago in his important book *God of the Oppressed*. He was responding to critics who objected to his claim that the right place to start our theological thinking is with the hermeneutical key that God is on the side of the oppressed. In response, Dr. Cone said that if the Bible did not teach that God is on the side of the oppressed, then he would either stop being a Christian or change his starting point.[7] In other words, the Bible was Cone's final authority. But in fact, Cone was right. The Bible does teach us in hundreds of places that God is on the side of the poor and the oppressed. Therefore, God's faithful people must do the same.

One of the great tragedies of the past half century is that so many preachers, especially white evangelical preachers, have not talked nearly as much about the poor as the Bible does. I think that has been a heretical failure. There are more verses in the Bible about God and the poor than about Jesus' resurrection. Yet evangelicals would say, and I agree, that ignoring or denying Jesus' bodily resurrection is heresy. Surely, then, denying or ignoring the even more frequent biblical statements about God being on the side of the poor is also tragic and terrible heresy.

Second, sin is both personal and social or structural. Somehow, it is much easier for many Christians to respond to social problems, whether poverty or racism, in individualistic, personal ways, rather than in structural ways. The famous Brazilian bishop Hélder Câmara said, "When I feed the hungry, they call me a saint. When I ask why they are hungry, they call me a communist."[8]

I was in India some decades ago, and I heard the following story from an Indian bishop. He said there was an insane asylum that had a very interesting way to decide if someone was well enough to go home. Apparently they would take a big tub over to a water tap, fill the tub up with water, and leave the tap running. Then they would give the person a spoon and say, "Please empty the tub." If the person started emptying the tub one spoonful at a time and never turned off the tap, they knew the person was still crazy. So often Christians go at social problems one spoonful at a time.

Books have been written about the fact that white Christians, especially white evangelicals, fail to understand the structural foundations of injustice and fail to embrace structural solutions. In the last part of my presentation, I want to apply these two biblical principles, especially the importance of structural change, to four areas: health care, our educational system, economic inequality, and Black Lives Matter. In each case, I do not want to embrace any narrowly partisan agenda. Debate about the best, most effective ways to solve our problems is good for democracy. But biblical Christians must demand that our country embrace just, effective solutions.

First, health care. Health care for everyone is a pro-life issue. Many studies have shown that people without access to health insurance have poorer health and die younger. Every pro-life person, every person who believes that each person is made in the image of God and therefore is immeasurably valuable, every person who accepts the biblical teaching that God has a special concern for the poor—every such person should be a leader in the struggle to demand universal health insurance for every person in the richest nation on earth. There is more than one way to reach that goal. I am glad to listen to various political proposals that would truly help us reach that goal. There are obvious weaknesses in former president Barack Obama's Affordable Care Act, but it is a fact that last year (2016) the number of those without health insurance dropped to 8.8 percent. That was the lowest rate of uninsured Americans in our history. Or, to put it positively, in 2016, more Americans had health insurance than at any time in our history.[9]

It is important for us to explore a variety of ways to fix the weaknesses in the present system and reach 100 percent coverage. But it is simply not pro-life, and it is unbiblical, to suggest and support proposals that result in millions more Americans losing health insurance. If they want to be biblical, white evangelicals must be among the leaders saying that loudly and clearly.

Second, education. Everybody knows that our inner-city schools are failing millions of Black, Hispanic, and yes, poor white children too. Everybody also knows that largely white suburban school districts typically offer much better education. That is one major reason why white Americans for decades, and now Black middle-class professionals as well, move to the suburbs. As Jesse Jackson said some time ago, some of our schools prepare people for Yale, others for jail. We all know that the causes of our troubled inner-city schools are complex. But we also know some things that would help. We could at least spend as much money per student on inner-city systems as on suburban ones. We could make it more attractive for our best teachers to teach in schools where students need the most help. Again, we can debate the most effective concrete ways to reach our goal of quality education for everyone. But for biblical people, that goal is not negotiable. White evangelical Christians ought to be among the leaders lobbying their white suburban politicians to make the necessary changes in funding and redistricting. That battle is surely one of the great civil rights issues of our time.

Third, the economy. Let's consider the fact that economic inequality in the US is greater today than at any time since just before the Great Depression in 1928. The richest 1 percent of Americans own more wealth than everyone in the bottom 90 percent. And the distribution of wealth has a clear racial side. The average white household has thirteen times as much wealth as the average African American household. In 2004 the richest 0.1 percent (that's one-tenth of 1 percent) had more combined pretax income than the poorest 120 million Americans. That means that if you divided the total US income among 1,000 people, the richest person would have as much income as the poorest 387. And as the economy grows, most of the increase goes to the richest 1 percent. In the last several years, over 90 percent of all the growth in the economy has gone to the richest 1 percent.[10]

Now, I do not think that biblical faith calls for absolute equality where every person has the same income and wealth. But biblical principles lead to two tests for whether the differences of wealth are too great. The first is this: Does the inequality of wealth help and encourage or hinder and prevent measures that would empower poor people to move out of poverty? The second is that in a sinful world, power tends to corrupt and absolute power corrupts absolutely. So, if a small group of people have vast economic wealth and power, they will almost certainly use it to benefit themselves rather than to empower poor people. And that is exactly what we see in the United States today. Many, although not all, very wealthy multimillionaires use their money to buy elections and push legislation that will reduce their taxes. And they fight against measures designed to empower poor people: whether health insurance for all, a higher minimum wage for low-income workers, more funds for inner-city schools, or foreign economic aid to fight poverty around the world. One current illustration is the proposal to give huge tax cuts to the richest persons, even though this will both significantly expand the federal debt and substantially reduce funds to empower poor people.

Again, there is room for honest debate and disagreement about what specific government proposals are wise and effective. But the starting point for anyone who claims to be a Christian must be this: Will this legislation empower or hurt the poorest 50 percent?

Finally, Black Lives Matter. Of course white lives matter too. Of course, blue lives matter as well. The life of every person is equally treasured by God.

But today's data is painfully clear. Evidence demonstrates that police more frequently kill Black men than white men. And again, and again, the best evidence shows that the lethal action taken by the police (and it is usually white police) was not justified. The broader statistics about our prisons also tell a wrenching story. Something is very wrong when African American men are imprisoned at a rate 5.1 times higher than white men. Something is wrong when African Americans are 12.6 percent of the total population but 38 percent of the prison population.[11]

At this time in this nation when racism is resurgent and open expression of racism is clearly if indirectly tolerated at the highest levels, it is crucial that white Christians—yes, white evangelicals—take the lead in helping white America face the painful fact of continuing racism in our society. White pastors must dare to lead their congregations to talk about and work courageously against the real racism that continues in America. It should become just as unacceptable in the white evangelical world to remain silent in the face of racism as it is unacceptable to endorse widespread abortion or blatant adultery. Studies make it painfully clear that racist attitudes are more prevalent in the white evangelical world than elsewhere. Unless white evangelicals and their leaders act vigorously to change that sinful fact, we will be like the earlier evangelical leaders who promoted so-called biblical arguments to justify slavery.

You and I live at an enormously critical historical moment. Fundamental issues of racial and economic justice are at stake. I hope and pray that Christian leaders will speak and act boldly to lead us away from the precipice and bring us to a better future. I even hope and pray for, and intend to do all I can to nurture, a situation where white evangelical leaders play a courageous, important role in leading this nation closer to that beloved community where racial and economic justice blesses everyone.

Notes

1. Martin Luther King Jr., "Letter from Birmingham Jail" (April 16, 1963), Liberation Curriculum, Martin Luther King, Jr. Papers Project, The Estate of Martin Luther King, Jr., 2004, https://kinginstitute.stanford.edu/sites/mlk/files/letterfrombirmingham_wwcw_0.pdf.

2. Christian Churches Together in the U.S.A., "A Response to Dr. Martin Luther King Jr.'s 'Letter from Birmingham Jail,'" April 16, 2013, https://static1.squarespace.com/static/5db60dcb78edb86950c818a0/t/5e56830e8ac092631b0edd7c/1582727951299/CCT+Response+to+Letter+From+Birmingham+Jail.pdf, accessed June 21, 2021.

3. King, "Letter from Birmingham Jail," 1.

4. King, 1.

5. King, 6–7.

6. King, 8.

7. James H. Cone, *God of the Oppressed* (New York: Seabury, 1975).

8. Hélder Câmara, as quoted in John Dear's *Peace Behind Bars: A Peacemaking Priest's Journal from Jail* (New York: Sheed & Ward, 1995), 65.

9. See https://www.kff.org/uninsured/issue-brief/key-facts-about-the-uninsured-population/.

10. See https://inequality.org/facts/income-inequality/.

11. See https://www.sentencingproject.org/publications/color-of-justice-racial-and-ethnic-disparity-in-state-prisons/.

PART 2
Sermons

CHAPTER 12

Praying for Peace and Justice

This is a sermon I prepared in the early 1980s and preached more than twenty times over the next two decades in North America, England, New Zealand, and Israel. In the last three decades since the collapse of the Soviet Union, the threat of nuclear holocaust has seemed to be significantly reduced. But that may be largely a failure to think carefully about the continuing expansion of countries with nuclear weapons.

The next two decades are the most dangerous in human history. I believe that the only hope for our time is a new movement of biblical Christians who immerse their search for peace and justice in prayer and the presence of the Holy Spirit.

Nuclear disarmament, the preservation of the family, international economic justice, prevention of environmental disaster, and the restoration of the sacredness of human life will involve fundamental changes in our society. But there is no way that will happen, no way to avoid global disaster in the next few decades, unless God sends sweeping revival and Spirit-breathed action for peace and justice. Prayer has always been central to mighty movements of God. I am sure it still is.

There have been important social movements in my lifetime, and many Christians have been involved in them. But never in recent times (except for the civil rights movement led by the Black church) has there been a movement calling for fundamental social change that was immersed in intercessory prayer and a radical dependence on the Holy Spirit. It is a tragic fact that contemporary Christian social activists place less emphasis on prayer than do their counterparts doing evangelism. Richard Lovelace is right: "Most of those who are praying are not praying about social issues, and most of those who are active in social issues are not praying very much."[1]

Earlier Models

That was not always the case. William Wilberforce and the other members of the Clapham Sect were the leaders in the great British crusade to abolish the slave trade and slavery itself. Historians tell us that they immersed their political strategizing and lobbying in daily three-hour sessions of intercessory prayer. Later in the nineteenth century, Lord Shaftesbury spearheaded a large number of social reforms, ending child labor and reforming factories. When his son asked him how he could do so many things at once, he replied, "By hearty prayer to Almighty God before I begin, by entering into it with faith and zeal, and by making my end to be His glory and the good of mankind."[2]

Charles Finney was the Billy Graham of the nineteenth century, but he was also one of the leading crusaders against slavery. Finney insisted that long hours of intercessory prayer were central to his work. Finney would have appreciated what German theologian Helmut Thielicke has said of Martin Luther. He prayed four hours each day, "not despite his busy life, but because only so could he accomplish his gigantic labors."[3]

The Promise of Jesus

If we are to learn how to pray, we must come to believe that Jesus meant what he said about prayer. Most Christians do not believe Jesus' teaching about prayer. And when I read his words, I can hardly blame them! Jesus said some of the most astonishing, outrageous things in his sayings on prayer. Listen to a few of them.

In Mark 11:23-24 (NIV), we have these incredible words: "Truly I tell you, if anyone says to this mountain, 'Go throw yourself into the sea,' and does not doubt in their heart but believes that what they say will happen, it will be done for them. Therefore, I tell you, whatever you ask for in prayer, believe that you have received it, and it will be yours."

When the disciples could not heal the boy with epilepsy, they asked Jesus for an explanation. Jesus pointed directly to their weak faith. "Truly I tell you, if you have faith as small as a mustard seed, you can say to this mountain, 'Move from here to there,' and it will move. Nothing will be impossible for you" (Matthew 17:20-21, NIV).

The Gospel of John contains this breathtaking promise: "Very truly I tell you, whoever believes in me will do the works I have been doing, and they will do even greater things than these, because I am going to the Father. And I will do whatever you ask in my name, so that the Father may be glorified in the Son. You may ask me anything in my name, and I will do it" (John 14:12-14, NIV).

"If you remain in me and my words remain in you, ask whatever you wish, and it will be done for you" (John 15:7, NIV).

Of course, none of us really believe him! He must be exaggerating! For years I never really took these promises of Jesus seriously. For years I didn't really believe he could have meant what he said. Slowly, however, I am beginning to think that perhaps he did.

My faith is still small, but it is growing. I am beginning to take seriously the fact that the One I confess to be God incarnate again and again said that whatever we ask in his name he will give. If we truly believe that the Carpenter from Nazareth was God in the flesh, then it is a very serious matter to doubt his oft-repeated promise that he will answer our prayers.

Three Conditions

Notice, however, that Jesus attached three important conditions to his promises. First, we must have faith. But that condition seems like a further burden rather than a help. If I don't have faith, I cannot suddenly manufacture it.

How do we obtain the necessary faith? I still feel very much a first-grader in the school of prayer. But two things have helped me at this point. In the past few years, I have struggled and cried to the Lord for the healing of broken marriages of close friends. And God has answered some of those prayers. As God did that, my faith has grown stronger. Furthermore, just remembering that it is my Lord who tells me that he will answer my prayer has also strengthened my faith.

I was meditating on Matthew 17:19-21 just after the anniversary of the Hiroshima bombing this year, pondering Jesus' promise that faith the size of a mustard seed would move mountains. Like a flash, the thought came: "Even, Lord, the prevention of nuclear war?"

That seemed too much! The nuclear arms race and the growing danger of nuclear holocaust is surely the most foreboding mountain looming over humanity today.

But the answer came back clearly: "Yes, even the mountain of nuclear weapons. Even that immovable mountain can be removed, if my people pray." I believe Jesus means exactly what he says. And he is the Lord of the universe. Surely, then, we can believe that the terrible mountain of nuclear weapons will be removed if God's people will unite in persistent, believing prayer.

But there is a second condition attached to Jesus' promise. We must be ready to obey. He said in John 15:7, "If you remain in me and my words remain in you, ask whatever you wish, and it will be done for you." Jesus makes this sweeping promise to answer prayer only to those who walk in intimate obedient fellowship with him. We abide in him as we commune daily with him. We abide in him as we keep his commandments. One of his commandments is that we forgive others with the same reckless abandon as he forgives us. Jesus insisted that when we start to pray, we must first forgive others (Mark 11:25).

It is impossible to pray properly with resentment in our hearts toward other people. My wife and I had a quarrel one weekend. When I started to prepare this piece on prayer the following Monday morning, I still felt anger and resentment toward Arbutus. I wanted to pray for God's guidance and help in the writing. But it quickly became clear that I first had to let go of my anger toward my wife before I could open myself in believing prayer for God's presence and direction. Obedience is inseparable from effectual prayer (James 5:16; 1 John 3:21-22). If we want to pray for peace and justice, we will also have to obey Jesus' command to be peacemakers and seekers of justice. If we want to pray for peace, we must let go of anger and hostility toward people of other nations.

A third condition is that our sole aim be to glorify God. Jesus says that whatever we ask in his name, he will do it. Why? So that the Father is glorified (John 14:12-14). That means that God will not answer self-seeking prayers. Our intention must be for God to be glorified. A central goal of the new movement for peace and justice must be the glory of God.

Prayer in Peacemaking

If we start to believe Jesus' promises about prayer and begin to fulfill the conditions attached to them, then the importance of prayer will become clearer and clearer to us. Prayer is a central way to work for peace and justice today. Prayer is not just something we do for our personal spiritual growth. Prayer is not merely a brief introductory invocation while the last persons straggle into the planning meeting for the nuclear freeze campaign.

Prayer is the way we do our work. Prayer is the way we change the world. God in his sovereignty has decided that our prayers affect history.

In his book *With Christ in the School of Prayer*, Andrew Murray said that in prayer we are allowed to hold the hand that holds the destiny of the universe. Christians, by their prayers, are "to determine the history of this earth."[4]

God wants to save the family. God wants more justice in society. God does not want to see God's beautiful creation destroyed in a nuclear holocaust or by massive global pollution. And God wants to accomplish those things through our prayers.

How incredible! Prayer is not incidental to peacemaking. Prayer is not peripheral to seeking justice for the oppressed. Prayer is a central part of how we do those things.

Andrew Murray put it well, "As long as we look on prayer chiefly as the means of maintaining our own Christian life, we shall not know fully what it is meant to be. But when we learn to regard it as the highest part of the work entrusted to us, the root and strength of all other work, we shall see that there is nothing that we so need to study and practice as the art of praying aright."[5]

Spiritual Warfare

Another reason prayer is so central to the search for peace and justice is that the battle is also a spiritual one. We are not just dealing with fearful politicians and selfish business leaders. We are also fighting against the demonic powers of Satan who want to destroy God's good creation (Ephesians 6:12). Only by spiritual warfare, only by the power of the Holy Spirit sought through intercessory prayer, can we overcome militarism, injustice, and the disintegration of the family.

Some Practical Suggestions

Reading a couple classics on prayer is a good place to start. Richard Foster's *Celebration of Discipline* is my first recommendation. Don't just read his book as an academic exercise; begin to apply his suggestions. Then follow Foster with Andrew Murray's *With Christ in the School of Prayer*.

For me, setting aside time at the beginning of the day has been important. You may want to start with ten minutes and work up to thirty to forty-five minutes. Don't be legalistic. It doesn't matter if you miss a day. But if you discover that you are only finding time once a week, then you know legalism is not your problem!

For years I struggled and fought with my busy schedule. Every morning the pile of "important, urgent" things was so great that I could hardly force myself to spare ten minutes to read and pray. Even when I did, my mind was preoccupied with the waiting responsibilities. Then the Lord allowed me to experience a very painful, difficult period in my life. The only way I survived was through crying out with agonized tears to the Lord. Those times of prayer, of telling God about my struggle, were times of deep comfort. As a result, I came to enjoy that daily conversation with my Lord in a way I never had before. During that time, and since, it has not been nearly so hard to set aside significant time at the beginning of the day for prayer and Bible reading.

Of course, our whole day of activity should be a life of prayer in which we pray without ceasing. And it also is wonderful to learn how to live at two levels. At one level we can be talking with friends or colleagues at work; at another level we can be breathing short prayers to God for ourselves and others. But it is still true—at least for me—that nothing takes the place of regular times set aside exclusively for conversation with our Divine Lover.

Breath prayers can also be helpful. In his book *The Breath of Life*, Ron DelBene suggests that each person select a short one-sentence prayer that they breathe to God many times each day. This prayer should focus on a central desire and concern in your life.[6] During lulls at work or school, or while driving or eating, you can breathe your short prayer to God. I wish Christians in the peace movement would adopt a breath prayer like the following: "Lord Jesus, please remove the mountain of nuclear weapons." Ask yourself what God would do if a few million Christian peace-makers breathed that prayer to God a dozen times a day for the next twenty years.

A personal conversation with David Watson, a leading British evangelist, provides another practical suggestion for the biblical movement of peace and justice today. When I talked with him a few years ago, he said God had led him to pray daily for the gift of evangelism. And God has answered that prayer in a marvelous fashion. David told me that he believed I should pray regularly for the gift of Spirit-filled work for peace and justice. I wish that every Christian concerned with peace and justice would do the same. Only God knows what a few million Spirit-filled, biblical peace-makers and social activists would accomplish by God's grace in the next two decades.

In our personal prayer, we should pray for specific things in the area of peace and justice. Daily let's ask the Sovereign of history to restrain the powers that want to destroy God's lovely creation in nuclear holocaust or environmental devastation. Let's pray for reconciliation between Christians, Jews, and Arabs in the Middle East. Let's pray for an end to starvation and a more just international economic order.

Group prayer is also important. More and more local groups of Christians are working for peace and justice across the land. I dream of each of these groups learning in a new way how to immerse their common activity in hours of intercessory prayer. In our committee meetings devoted to mapping out strategy, could we devote half as much time to seeking guidance from the King in prayer as we do in discussion with each other?

A New Praying Movement

Imagine a local group working to abolish nuclear weapons or to demand a living wage. The most sophisticated strategy and hard work would be combined with long sessions of group prayer as well as private prayer by all the individuals involved. At particularly important times when key decisions needed to be made, there would be all-night prayer chains. During the time when some members visited the mayor for support, others would gather to pray. On the night before the election, prayer chains would intercede throughout the night for the transforming presence of the Holy Spirit.

The same sense of prayer and radical dependence on the Holy Spirit would pervade regional and national peace and justice conferences. Surely, we are not too secular to make our conferences on peace and justice a little more like the old camp meetings where Christians interceded all night (like Jesus) for the radicalizing presence of the Holy Spirit.

Prayer, I hope, will become the trademark of a new movement for peace and justice. If that happens, American society could recover a commitment to the sacredness of human life and the sanctity of the family. If that happens, affluent Americans could join the developing world in a new partnership for global justice. If that happens, our children could even be spared nuclear holocaust and devastating climate change.

But that will happen only if each of us, one by one, resolves to draw nearer to God. That will happen only if each of us understands that at the center of Christian faith is a personal living relationship with the risen Lord. That will happen only if each of us nurtures that relationship with God in Christ through regular prayer and costly obedience. As that happens, you and I, through our prayers, can change the course of world history. Let's seize the missing link of prayer, believing that it is as strong as Jesus said it is.

To those who believe and pray, all things are possible.

Lord, I believe; help thou my unbelief.

Notes

1. Richard Lovelace, *Dynamics of Spiritual Life: An Evangelical Theology of Renewal* (Downers Grove, IL: InterVarsity, 1979), 392.

2. Lovelace, 381–82.

3. Quoted in Elton Trueblood, *The New Man for Our Time* (New York: Harper & Row, 1970), 66–67.

4. Andrew Murray, *With Christ in the School of Prayer: Thoughts on Our Training for the Ministry of Interession* (Old Tappan, NJ: Revell, 1953), 102–3.

5. Murray, 8.

6. Ron DelBene, *The Breath of Life: A Simple Way to Pray* (Eugene, OR: Wipf and Stock, 2005).

CHAPTER 13

Jubilee: Then and Now

I preached this sermon on June 7, 1985, in Düsseldorf, West Germany, at the 1985 Deutscher Evangelischer Kirchentag, a biannual event of the German Protestant Church, regularly bringing together about a hundred thousand participants. The themes developed here have been central to my thinking about economic justice for virtually all of my life.

"Then have the trumpet sounded everywhere on the tenth day of the seventh month; on the Day of Atonement sound the trumpet throughout your land. Consecrate the fiftieth year and proclaim liberty throughout the land to all its inhabitants. It shall be a jubilee for you; each of you is to return to your family property and to your own clan. . . .

"In this Year of Jubilee everyone is to return to their own property.

"If you sell land to any of your own people or buy land from them, do not take advantage of each other. You are to buy from your own people on the basis of the number of years since the Jubilee. And they are to sell to you on the basis of the number of years left for harvesting crops. When the years are many, you are to increase the price, and when the years are few, you are to decrease the price, because what is really being sold to you is the number of crops. Do not take advantage of each other, but fear your God. I am the LORD your God. . . .

"The land must not be sold permanently, because the land is mine and you reside in my land as foreigners and strangers. . . .

"If one of your fellow Israelites becomes poor and sells some of their property, their closest relative is to come and redeem what they have sold. If, however, there is no one to redeem it for them but later on they prosper and acquire sufficient means to redeem it themselves, they are to determine the value for the years since they sold it and refund the balance to the one to whom they sold it; they can then go back to their own property. But if they do not acquire the means to repay, what was sold will remain in the possession of the buyer until the Year of Jubilee. It will be returned in the Jubilee, and they can then go back to their property." (Leviticus 25:9-10, 13-17, 23, 25-28, NIV)

What an astonishing text! A dozen questions instantly flash across our minds. Is this text realistic or practical? Was it ever implemented? What is the date of this legislation? Unfortunately, we do not have the time this morning for all these important questions.

For our purposes, there is a sense in which the questions about date and implementation are not urgent. Regardless of the date of this legislation, regardless of whether Israel ever implemented it, it stands as part of the biblical canon confessed by Christians as God's Word. Christians over the centuries have confessed that the whole Bible is part of the church's authoritative canon. Christians believe that in some way that we do not fully understand, God speaks to us decisively from all parts of the Word of God.

Three questions are important for us: (1) What are the key proposals in the text? (2) What are the central principles that stand behind these proposals? (3) What is the meaning of this text for today?

First, the key proposals. Every fiftieth year is to be a Jubilee year in which all land returns to the original owners and all Hebrew slaves are freed. No payment is required. No questions are asked about why people lost their land or fell into slavery. On the fiftieth year, freedom reigns.

Before and after the fiftieth year of Jubilee, people can buy and sell land—or better, they can buy and sell the crops. Notice that the text explicitly says that God is the owner of all the land. Therefore, people can only buy the number of crops from the day of purchase to the day of the next Jubilee. And justice is crucial. You pay more if there are a lot of years for crops before the next Jubilee, and less if the years are few.

Notice, too, that there is a right of redemption for the person who has to sell land. People might sell their land because of desperate poverty due to anything from poor crops to natural disasters to laziness or poor management. As a result, they need immediate money to purchase food for the family. But if a person sells his land, then a close relative is obliged, if possible, to buy back the land for the poor person. Or if this does not happen and the person recovers financial stability, then the original owner has the right to go to the new owner and buy back the land. And the new owner must return it.

What a radical text. It is hardly surprising that there is little evidence to suggest that the Israelites ever regularly practiced this law. But even if they never had the courage and obedience to practice it, this text still stands as part of God's Word for God's people even today. To understand how to apply this part of God's Word, we need to explore our second question: What are the central principles that stand behind this astonishing text? There are at least six.

First, God is the only absolute owner. Absolute private ownership is forbidden because God alone is the only absolute owner. Verse 23 puts it bluntly: "The land must not be sold permanently, because the land is mine and you reside in my land as foreigners and strangers." The people who occupy the land are only temporary stewards, caring for the land for the true owner, Jehovah.

Since God owns it, God can demand that no matter how much interest you may have in making a perpetual profit, you must return it to the original owner at the Jubilee.

Second, it is clear that persons matter more than things or private ownership. The poor person's right to get the land back in order to be able to earn his own way is a higher right than the buyer's interest in making a profit.

Third, this text tells us that God demands something like equality of economic opportunity up to a significant degree. In the agricultural society presupposed in our text, land is the basic means of production. It is the basic capital. The assumption in the Pentateuch is that the land has been divided more or less equally among the tribes and families. This text says that God wants this basic means of production to go back to the original owners every fifty years. Some people may have more gifts or natural talents than others; some people may have more initiative and drive. As a result, some may produce more than others and be able to acquire more and more land. But God does not want these differing abilities to result in greater and greater extremes of wealth or poverty. Every fifty years, the basic means of production are to be returned to the original owners in order that a basic equality of economic opportunity (up to the point that everyone has the capital to earn a living) may prevail.

Fourth, this text clearly cares about the family. By giving each family the basis for an independent economic existence, God says loudly and clearly that God cares about the family as a central intermediate institution in society.

Fifth, this text demands personal economic responsibility. It does not call for a welfare system that makes an indefinite number of goods available regardless of people's personal choices. This text attempts to guarantee that every family has the economic means to stand on their own feet and earn their own way. If they make bad choices and fall into poverty, they will lose their land

and will have to work for other, more successful farmers for a time. Certainly, God insists that this dare not result in social classes divided by greater and greater extremes of wealth and poverty. Every seven years, Hebrew slaves are freed. And every fifty years every family gets their land back and has a new chance to be responsible and self-reliant. Personal economic responsibility to create wealth, not perpetual societal handouts, is central to the text.

Finally, Leviticus 25 calls for decentralized private ownership (or stewardship) of property, not state ownership or centralized private ownership. *Stewardship* is a better word than *ownership*, because God is the only absolute owner of the land. And God insists that property rights are severely limited. An absolute, unending right to own property indefinitely and use it in any way one pleases is totally foreign to this text. But the conclusion from this important limitation on private ownership in no way leads to state ownership of the land. Rather, this text calls for decentralized private ownership (or stewardship). Each family must have control over the means to earn their own way.

From other parts of biblical truth, we can see why this decentralized family ownership is so important. Both a positive and a negative reason are significant. Each person and family is called to be a co-shaper of history under God. Economics, of course, is a central part of human life. If the important economic decisions are centralized in a few hands, then most people are unable to be genuine coworkers with God in the shaping of history.

A negative reason is equally crucial. Because of human sinfulness, people tend to use power for their own selfish advantage. Power tends to corrupt, and absolute power tends to corrupt absolutely. Therefore, centralization of power is extremely dangerous. It almost inevitably leads to oppression and totalitarianism. Centralizing economic power and political power by placing ownership of the means of production in the state is therefore highly dangerous. Only decentralized economic stewardship of property provides a balance of power. And only thus can fallen people live together in society with a reasonable degree of freedom and harmonious interdependence.

We have discovered six important principles in this text:

1. God is the only absolute owner of property.
2. People matter more than property.
3. God demands something like equality of economic opportunity up to the point where everyone has the opportunity to earn a decent living.
4. God cares about the family as a central intermediate institution in society.
5. God wants families to be responsible and self-reliant creators of wealth.
6. God wants decentralized private ownership, not centralized ownership by the state or small elites.

What do these principles mean for us today? They are relevant first to the church and then to the larger society. Because of limitations of time, however, I will speak only about the second area.

It would be absurd to try to apply the specific mechanism of the Jubilee in today's complex global economy. Western colonial masters who owned a good deal of the earth fifty years ago would get a lot of land back! God's word to Israel was a divine disclosure of how Israelite society should be shaped for the sake of justice and shalom. It is the basic paradigm of that divine revelation that must be applied today. To the extent that contemporary societies implement the basic principles of God's revelation about shalom, they will be just, creative, and peaceful.

I want to emphasize three areas where the biblical paradigm needs to be applied to our complex world: (1) the centrality of the family; (2) the lack of equality of economic opportunity in today's polarized world; and (3) the debate between communism and capitalism.

God wants the family to be a self-reliant, responsible social institution standing on its own feet and earning its own way. That means that the state ought not to intervene in the family except in extreme situations. The family, not the state, has the basic responsibility for the rearing of children. Public policy should strengthen, not weaken, lifelong marriage covenant and parental responsibility for children.

A welfare system that dooms some families to a permanent situation of dependency on public handouts for their basic livelihood is not God's will. Of course, that does not mean public measures such as state health insurance, unemployment insurance, and aid to the needy are wrong. Thank God for such provisions. But it does mean that both nationally and internationally, families and nations need to be empowered to earn their own way rather than depend on permanent government handouts. Permanently depending on public welfare creates a debilitating dependency that is destructive both for individuals and families and also for the larger society. We need private and public initiatives to empower families to earn their own way rather than more programs that make people permanently dependent on the state.

Equality of economic opportunity is central to the promotion of self-reliant, responsible families. A hasty glance at the division of our global village into extremely wealthy and extremely poor quickly shows how far we are from equality of economic opportunity.

That is not to say that there ought to be some modern egalitarian, absolute equality of consumption. Nor is it to suppose that economics is a zero-sum game where one person can acquire wealth only at the expense of others. The wealth of the West, Japan, Singapore, and Australia is not all due to oppression and injustice. Hard work, biblical values regarding the material world and history, and creative ideas are crucial factors in the creation of wealth. On the other hand, I do not for a moment overlook the role of colonialism, slavery, and economic oppression in the creation of some of the wealth of the West.

But no matter how one analyzes the relative importance of oppressive colonialism on the one hand and creative ingenuity on the other in the creation of Western wealth, it is still the case that this Jubilee text calls for something like equality of economic opportunity to a significant degree. And that means sweeping change. Jubilee was a societal mechanism designed to guarantee that everybody regularly received the means to earn their own way. Christians today who want to practice what the Bible preaches must demand and model a massive redistribution of the world's productive resources. Nothing less than that kind of sweeping empowerment of the poor to enable them to earn their own way is faithful to God's revealed Word.

In many parts of the world, land is still a major means of production. To enable the agricultural masses to stand on their own feet, there must be major land reform. Each farming family needs enough land to earn their own way, plus the appropriate tools, credit, and seeds to make that land productive.

In our technological world, knowledge is a major source of productivity. Sharing universal quality education and appropriate technology is a central way to implement the Jubilee.

I'm a theologian, not an economist or politician, so I do not presume to have a detailed blueprint for sharing the world's resources in such a way that everyone has the opportunity to earn their own way. But Christian economists and political scientists must design the detailed agendas, and all of us must work for their implementation. The goal is the Jubilee vision of significant equality of economic opportunity for every family.

Finally, we need to ask briefly whether our text has anything to say about the competing ideologies of communism and laissez-faire capitalism. I think it rejects both and demands a third way.

Our text knows nothing of some absolute right of private property. It soundly condemns a concern to maximize profits regardless of the impact on people. Justice, not mere supply and demand, must shape economic life.

On the other hand, there is no hint in our text of the communist ideal of state ownership of the bulk of the means of production. Both biblical principles and the history of communist totalitarianism warn us against centralizing economic power and political power in the state. No fallen man or woman can use that kind of power justly. Biblical faith points us in the direction of decentralized private ownership of land, banking, and industrial production.

This principle, of course, includes a mandate for change, not just in the East but also in the West. The concentration of vast economic power in the hands of small elites that control large multinational corporations also represents a dangerous concentration of power. The political power of those who control our five hundred largest multinational corporations is enormous. Why people who denounce the communist centralization of power overlook this similar, likewise dangerous concentration of power is puzzling when it is not amusing.

To call for decentralized economic structures is not to suppose that we can or should return to the cottage industry of the Middle Ages. Our best scientists and scholars will have to figure out how to promote genuinely decentralized ownership and control of our complex, technological economic world. But unless we do that, we are doomed to experience a future full of totalitarian oppression. The only alternative is to dare by God's grace to implement a contemporary equivalent of the Jubilee vision.

In conclusion, I want to call attention to one part of the text that I have ignored. Verse 9 says that the Year of Jubilee begins on the Day of Atonement. Now, that is very significant. The Day of Atonement was the annual festival in Israel in which offerings

206

were made for the sins of the people. It was the day on which sinful Israel's right relationship with their holy God was renewed.

It is highly significant that the Jubilee year, which was a radical restoration of right relationships on the horizontal human level, begins on the Day of Atonement, the day when vertical right relationships are restored. That points to the fact that right relationships with neighbor are impossible finally without a right relationship with God.

Modern thought suggests otherwise. Since the eighteenth century, we have been told that if we just change the social environment, we can create a new, better person. Marxism naively tells us that if we can only rid ourselves of private property, we will create a new humanity and a new utopian society. That is naive, dangerous nonsense. The human problem is deeper than social structures. To be sure, it is very important to correct unjust social systems. But the human problem lies much deeper. The heart of the human dilemma is humanity's proud rebellion against God. When we tried to run our lives by our own standards rather than submit to God's truth, we not only sinned against the Creator but also produced sin, agony, and hell in human relationships—lying, adultery, economic oppression, war.

If the source of the problem is rebellion against God, then the solution is repentance and a return to obedience. No human schemes for a more just society will be permanently and largely successful unless they are grounded in changed persons transformed by a living relationship with God in Christ.

That is why evangelism must be a central part of a biblical movement of social change. Western oppressors need to be transformed by a living relationship with Jesus Christ. Only then will they be ready to share gladly in redistribution of resources so there may be equality of opportunity. Oppressed peasants need to be transformed by a living encounter with a God who loved them so much that he came to die for them on the cross. Only then will they develop the self-respect and dignity necessary to demand a just role in the shaping of society.

Christians who become so preoccupied with social change that they lose their passion for prayer, worship, and sharing the gospel are not only unfaithful to Jesus but also undercut the very foundation for fundamental social change.

Jubilee begins on the Day of Atonement. Right relationship with neighbor is grounded in right relationship with God. Lasting social change requires evangelism.

This world needs to be changed. The poor cry out to you and me for justice. To respond to their plea, you and I must cry out to the living God for forgiveness and transformation. Let's throw ourselves into the exciting struggle to implement the Jubilee vision. And let's do so in the power of the risen Lord Jesus. Amen.

CHAPTER 14

Evangelical Pastors
and the Poor

I presented this message more than four dozen times,
often as part of a longer presentation on global poverty,
to pastors, seminary students, and church leaders in
North America, Europe, Australia, Japan, and South
Korea in the years 1986–2007.

I once met a pastor who frankly told me, "I agree with you that
the Bible says a great deal about God and the poor, but I simply
cannot preach that to my congregation. They would not tolerate
that." I am afraid many pastors feel somewhat that way.

Usually, of course, this sentiment is not put so directly. But it
always scares me. I wonder who is lord of that leader. I wonder,
too, if they truly believe in the Holy Spirit and the Word of God.
I have a very high view of the power of the preached Word and
the work of the Holy Spirit. I believe the Reformers were right:
when God's Word is faithfully preached, the Holy Spirit is mightily at work overcoming barriers, breaking down resistance, and
nurturing new openness.

It is possible to faithfully preach what the Bible says about the
poor and not get thrown out. I know successful pastors who are
doing it. Recently I was in a five-thousand-member Pentecostal
church. The senior pastor is skillfully, prayerfully, in the power of
the Holy Spirit leading that huge congregation into a new understanding of ministry to the poor. He had just preached a sermon

on Isaiah 58. He used the catchy title "Fasting without Giving Up Food." I know successful pastors who wisely combine firsthand exposure to third-world poverty with their teaching and preaching. Don't let anybody tell you that you must choose between pastoral failure and biblical obedience when it comes to teaching about the poor.

On the other hand, I don't mean to be blind to the difficulties. We all know that the current climate in our society and churches is not an ideal one for preaching on Amos. A heretical gospel of wealth is alive and well. Many of our people prefer comforting sermons to biblical fidelity. College and university students may come to church, but they want to be reassured that their preoccupation with good grades so they can get excellent jobs and enjoy an affluent lifestyle is pleasing to almighty God. We live in a self-indulgent, materialistic time. It won't be easy and you will pay a price if you choose to preach what the Bible says about the poor.

Literally hundreds of verses in the Bible talk about God's special concern for the poor. In chapter 3 of my book *Rich Christians in an Age of Hunger*, I show that God insists that God's people share God's concern for the poor. If they do not, the Bible suggests, they may not truly be God's people, no matter how orthodox their theology or how intense their worship.

If you intend to be biblical as a pastor or Christian leader, you will need to decide that no matter what the cost, you will insist on teaching and preaching about justice for the poor just as much as the Bible does. You will need to insist that the local congregations you pastor or the organizations you lead reexamine their total ministry—their missions giving, their construction plans, their Sunday school and adult teaching curricula—to make sure the congregation or organization is just as concerned about justice for the poor as God is. Anything less would be not only heresy but also a rejection of Jesus Christ as Lord. If you are afraid to teach or preach justice for the poor the way the Bible does, then you are denying Christ just as surely as the atheist. You have four options.

First, the *radical option*. You can preach five fiery sermons and get thrown out. Second is the *conformist option*. You can calculate what the people want to hear and preach that always, of course, throwing in an annual sermon on the poor on World Hunger Sunday to silence your conscience. Both of these first two options are wrong. I hope they don't tempt anyone who tries to submit to the authority of the Scriptures.

The third option is the *calculating option*. If you decide to lead your congregation into greater faithfulness toward the poor, you calculate how much they can take, and you do that, pushing courageously at least occasionally to the limit of their goodwill and tolerance. But you never go beyond what they will accept without deep anger. You never put your job at risk. Of course you never say it that way. You always tell yourself that your cautious, slow approach is only so that you can carry everyone along. But in spite of your genuine desire to be biblical, the bottom line is really a careful calculation of what the market will bear. I'm afraid the calculating option is really only a more sophisticated version of the conformist option.

The fourth possibility is a Spirit-filled, *costly option*. You can decide that you would rather have Jesus than parsonage and pulpit or presidency. You can decide that over the course of the next five years, you will develop a comprehensive program of preaching, teaching, and experience that will expose your people to the full biblical Word about God's concern for the poor. Certainly, you will be a gentle pastor, a listening counselor, an orthodox teacher, an eager evangelist. But you will also be a courageous prophet. You will organize tours for key leadership to rural Central America and inner-city America.

Over the course of those five years, you will offer the best program you know how to develop to give your congregation the best possible opportunities to hear in a favorable way the biblical call for justice for the poor. But you will not back down. You will not water down the message to mollify corporate executives, affluent professionals, or wealthy farmers. You will be faithful to the full biblical Word no matter what the cost. Christ, not ecclesiastical advance or church growth, will be your Lord.

Do you know what will happen if you take this fourth option? You may get thrown out when your congregation realizes that you are serious. But I believe that very frequently, the Holy Spirit will convert hard hearts and transform stubborn materialists, and you will see surprising revival and transformed lives. The Spirit is alive and well, working mightily when we preach the Word faithfully. If you resolve to tell your future congregations everything the Bible says about God's concern for the poor, you can expect that again and again God will reward your obedience with biblically compassionate, growing congregations and organizations.

But not always. You must be ready to fail in human terms. Unless you are ready to risk getting thrown out, you will never dare to preach the full biblical Word. And that will mean that no matter how you rationalize it, no matter how you massage your conscience, you really worship job security more than Jesus.

The ultimate question is really very simple: Who is your Lord?

CHAPTER 15

A Tale of Two Churches

I preached this sermon in the chapel at Yale Divinity School in New Haven, Connecticut, on April 11, 2002. Tragically, so much of white evangelical social engagement in the last two decades focused on right-wing politics, ending up in the embrace of Donald Trump.

My first teaching position after I left Yale in 1968 was at a new inner-city campus of Messiah College, a small evangelical college in mid-Pennsylvania, which was setting up a second campus at the edge of Temple University in the midst of all-Black North Philadelphia. My family lived in North Philly for seven years, attending a Black church, integrating the local elementary school, and learning a great deal about the inner city.

One of the more exciting activities of those early years was a series of two-day, weekend seminars held in North Philly for white, suburban, rural and small-town church leaders. I was regularly amazed to see the change fostered by just two days of walking the streets, sleeping in neighborhood homes, and listening to half a dozen African American speakers.

Father Paul Washington and Rev. Willie Richardson almost always spoke to my weekend visitors. Father Washington was famous across Philadelphia and beyond for his daring, vigorous social engagement. A prominent civil rights leader and chair of the mayor's Human Relations Commission, Father Washington led his Episcopalian Church of the Advocate into a vast array of social ministries and work for justice. His church provided the location for the first ordination of women as Episcopalian priests. It also hosted the Black Panthers' Constitutional Convention in 1970. Mrs. Washington led the Advocate Community Development Corporation, which developed more than three hundred units of new or rehabilitated lower-income housing. Father Washington and his church had a major, positive impact on North Philadelphia, indeed the whole city and even the nation.

Members of Church of the Advocate still worship in their grand, cathedral-like stone structure that easily seats a thousand people. But for decades the congregation gathering each Sunday was a tiny group of fewer than one hundred worshipers. Today about sixty are present on a typical Sunday. Evangelism was not a significant concern for Father Washington, and his church paid almost no attention to it for decades. Slowly the congregation withered away.

When I first visited Rev. Willie Richardson's church in 1969, Christian Stronghold Baptist met in one room of a row house. Reverend Richardson was a full-time engineer, pastoring his little flock of fifty or so people in his spare time. But he was passionate about evangelism and discipleship, teaching all his members how to share their faith with others. Christian Stronghold is now a congregation of more than four thousand members, half of whom never belonged to any church at all before they joined Christian Stronghold. An extensive training program for new members nurtures a passion for evangelism in everyone.

"Everything we do is an evangelistic outreach," Richardson says. But that "everything" includes a vast amount of social ministry that has developed over the years: a GED program, hundreds of renovated low-income houses, home ownership seminars, health fairs, a youth self-esteem program for troubled students at a nearby elementary school, tutoring, and a Community Action Council working on political issues. Richardson has inspired his congregation to share his passion for both evangelism and social action.

In a recent survey of the congregation, we discovered that 82 percent of the respondents at Christian Stronghold reported leading someone to Christ, and 95 percent reported helping someone in need with food, clothing, or money in the previous twelve months. And 83 percent had helped someone find a job. Christian Stronghold Baptist Church offers a powerful example of our text from Matthew 9:35 (NIV): "Jesus went through all the towns and villages, teaching in their synagogues, proclaiming the good news of the kingdom, and healing every disease and sickness." Christian Stronghold combines evangelism and social action, loving the whole person the way Jesus did in a powerful expression of holistic ministry.

To a significant degree, the tale of these two congregations runs parallel to the story of the whole church and one of the great debates in the twentieth century. In the early years of the twentieth century, the social gospel movement emerged as a powerful voice for social engagement in the church. Walter Rauschenbusch's famous lectures here at Yale, published in 1917 as *A Theology for the Social Gospel*, became perhaps the most articulate manifesto for a sustained, creative movement that for decades battled economic injustice, strengthened unions, and eventually opposed racism. Rauschenbusch was right that traditional churches had too often understood both sin and salvation in one-sided individualistic ways, neglected structural injustice, and ignored Jesus' ethical teaching. The social gospel movement Rauschenbusch loved and led dramatically changed American society for the better.

Reading Rauschenbusch's *A Theology for the Social Gospel*, however, shows why those who stand in the mainstream of historic Christian orthodoxy were uneasy. He belittled "trust in the vicarious atonement of Christ," insisted that the social gospel had little interest in metaphysical questions about the Trinity or deity of Christ, and gladly predicted that "the more the Social Gospel engages and inspires theological thought, the more religion will be concentrated on ethical righteousness."[1]

That is, of course, exactly what happened. Many mainline Protestant congregations and denominations focused more and more on important issues of social justice, neglecting evangelism and church planting. In response, people who called themselves fundamentalists and then later evangelicals focused one-sidedly on evangelism and orthodox theology, largely neglecting what the Bible says about justice for the poor and marginalized. For decades this tragic division, debate, and one-sidedness weakened American church life. And for decades the stereotype persisted that mainline Protestants cared about social justice and evangelicals cared about evangelism.

Then the tale of the two churches took an interesting twist in the last few decades of the twentieth century. Thanks in part to the civil rights movement, the anti–Vietnam War campaign, and liberation theology, more and more younger evangelicals developed a passion for social justice, rediscovered the massive biblical teaching about God's special concern for the poor, and began to define the gospel not merely as the forgiveness of sins, but as the Good News of the kingdom. In the last three decades, more and more evangelical thinkers and congregations developed a vigorous commitment to social action while maintaining a passion for evangelism and a commitment to historic Christian orthodoxy. Scores of old, established congregations with a long history of missionary engagement slowly developed extensive social ministry programs, and hundreds of new evangelical congregations and ministries emerged with successful holistic ministries combining evangelism and social programs.

In 1998 the University of Chicago published a book called *American Evangelicalism: Embattled and Thriving*, written by University of North Carolina sociologist Christian Smith. Smith used a large national survey to show what had happened. Not surprisingly, his polling data showed that evangelicals were far more engaged in evangelism than mainline Protestants. But he also discovered that evangelicals were just as likely as mainline Protestants to vote in elections; evangelicals were more likely to consider working for political reform very important (69 percent) than mainline Protestants (53 percent); evangelicals were slightly more likely than mainline Protestants to consider volunteering for local community organizations (77 percent versus 73 percent); and evangelicals were more likely than mainline Protestants to have given a lot of money to help the poor and needy (29 percent versus 22 percent). Smith concluded that today "evangelicals may be the most committed carriers of a new Social Gospel."[2]

The national church story of the last few decades seems to be the story of Church of the Advocate and Christian Stronghold Baptist writ large. While mainline Protestant denominations have been losing millions of members, evangelical congregations and denominations have been growing rapidly, not just numerically but in their social engagement.

This tale of two churches prompts a question about the present society-wide debate about President George W. Bush's faith-based initiative. Which set of churches is more likely to produce ministries that foster long-term social change? Many Mainline Protestant congregations support a number of social ministries running a wide variety of important programs to care for and empower the poor. Often, however, the program content of these church-related social ministries is not much different from secular programs. Both simply offer a variety of socioeconomic inputs using the best of the medical and social sciences with little or no attention to spiritual transformation.

The growing number of holistic evangelical social programs on the other hand believe that the causes of poverty and social brokenness are both personal and structural, spiritual and social. Therefore, they not only use the best of the medical and social sciences but also emphasize prayer, evangelism, and the transforming power of the Holy Spirit. They believe that since persons are both social and spiritual beings, lasting social change will require both socioeconomic and also inner spiritual transformation. People, they believe, need Jesus *and* a job.

In the next decade, as the new interest in faith-based approaches unfolds, there will be sophisticated sociological studies by our best scholars comparing the success rates of different types of social service providers: secular providers; nominally religious providers run by churches with no substantial emphasis on spiritual transformation; and holistic Christian social service providers that include a great deal of emphasis on spiritual transformation combined with extensive socioeconomic change. It will be fascinating to see what the scholars discover.

A very recent development at Father Washington's Church of the Advocate suggests another interesting possibility. They have recently begun to explore ways of evangelizing their community. They realize that the hope of preserving their legacy of social action depends in part on sharing the gospel with others who will join the church and carry on the work. Perhaps the future will reveal a powerful convergence from both the right and the left of churches that embrace both Good News and good works.

I end with a story—a tale of two stages in the life of one Christian social program. In the early seventies, Glen and Lonni Kehrein launched a new Christian social ministry called Rock/Circle in one of the very poor sections of West Chicago. A graduate of Moody Bible Institute, Glen just assumed that evangelism would be an important part of his work. But he had no interest in pushing tracts down people's throats. He wanted his actions to prompt questions that could be answered with the gospel. Ten years later, Glen's ministry had a staff of twenty full-time workers running a number of social programs, including a medical clinic, low-income housing renovation, and a youth program.

As Glen reflected on their programs, however, he slowly realized that evangelism was not really happening in his programs and his programs were not making a long-term difference in people's lives. His philosophy had been, "Act out the gospel. Demonstrate it. People will see what we do and ask why we do it." The only problem, Glen now says, is that "not many people asked why we were doing what we were doing." Glen began to ask himself what criteria he should use to measure what he was doing. "Is it the number of buildings we rehab?" he wondered. Glen concluded that what he really wanted was not just rehabbed buildings but changed lives. Furthermore, he now says, "In the first ten years of our ministry, we didn't see very many lives changed."

At about this time, Raleigh Washington graduated from Trinity Evangelical Divinity School with a passion to do evangelism and church planting in some comfortable middle-class setting. But a friend introduced Raleigh to Glen, and God called this high-powered African American retired army officer to join Glen in the inner city. Raleigh began a series of evangelistic programs inter-laced throughout the social programs of Glen's successful commu-nity center. Slowly all the staff at the community center learned how to combine active relational evangelism with their social pro-grams. Over the second ten years of this ministry, hundreds of people came to faith in Christ and a thriving congregation of 350 people developed, worshiping each Sunday in the community cen-ter's gym. The social ministries continued to grow in the second ten years: an expanding medical clinic, a legal clinic, hundreds of renovated houses, small business development—all immersed in a gentle but passionate friendship evangelism.

Wanda Caldwell's story illustrates how this holistic ministry produces long-term transformation. Wanda first came to Rock/Circle in 1983. She was single, pregnant, only seventeen, and so scared she tried to commit suicide. Counselors at the com-munity center helped her through that crisis. A year later, after drugs and wild parties, she almost died with a ruptured stomach. Dr. Beran at the medical clinic prayed with her just before her surgery. But she returned to drugs and a wild life as a successful rock soloist.

At the height of her success, her life was in chaos. She used drugs regularly and often drank herself senseless. For twelve years she drove a car without a driver's license. She had all her utility bills in different names and was behind on all of them. She collected welfare even though she was paid fairly well for her music. Her boyfriend was trying to get her hooked on cocaine.

Through all these years, she attended different churches. But they never satisfied—or changed—her. At a moment of deep despair, her mother told her about the church called Rock that met in the community center's gym. Desperate, she decided to attend.

She arrived with her wild hairstyle and wild clothes. Her first surprise was to meet Dr. Beran, the doctor who had prayed with her before surgery. The love and warmth she felt on that first visit from the members of Rock Church overwhelmed her. "It was like the Spirit of the Lord engulfed me and hugged me." She decided to attend regularly.

Wanda found people at the church and community center ready to walk with her through her many problems. The medical clinic provided medical care and counseling for her and her children. Years of ignoring bills meant she was close to going to jail. The legal clinic helped, and the bill collectors were patient when she confessed. She got a driver's license.

Paul Grant, music minister at Rock Church and full-time chaplain at the community center, gently yet firmly walked with her through the painful, drastic changes she needed to make. Sometimes she wanted to throw things at Paul for his tough love. But he and others persisted. "They really had some patience," Wanda says. "If they had given up, I would probably still be out on the street, just as wild as anything that's out there right now. But they kept calling, kept holding on to me, kept hugging me, kept telling me that they loved me. I didn't think I was worthy to be loved that much."

Today Wanda and her happy children tell others about Christ. Recently she visited an old friend in the hospital. In earlier days, they used to "hang" together on the street. Then a bullet paralyzed him from the waist down. When she told him her story, her friend also accepted Christ.

God and God's faithful people have transformed Wanda. She is off welfare. She has a job to support her children. And she uses her gift of song to sing for the Lord. "I've come a long way," Wanda says.

Does anybody think that all Wanda Caldwell needed was a better welfare system, a good job training program, or an expanded earned income tax credit? Surely, she needed Jesus *and* a job.

Remember, Jesus, taught, healed, and proclaimed the Good News. We should do the same.

My prayer: "Somehow, please, God, may this generation of church leaders rediscover how to love the whole person the way Jesus did."

Notes

1. Walter Rauschenbusch, *A Theology for the Social Gospel* (Eastford, CT: Martino Fine Books, 2010).

2. Christian Smith, *American Evangelicalism: Embattled and Thriving* (Chicago: University of Chicago Press, 2010).

CHAPTER 16

Will You Be Any Different?

This is my commencement address at Messiah College,
Dillsburg, Pennsylvania, on May 16, 2009.

President Phipps, faculty colleagues, graduates, family, and
friends:

Graduates, my question for you this morning is very simple:
"Will you be any different?"

Whenever I think carefully about Christian faith, I am utterly
amazed. Modern science continues to disclose the breathtaking
vastness and astonishing complexity of our fourteen-billion-year-
old universe with its one hundred-plus billion galaxies, each with
its own billions of stars. Christian faith tells us that at the center
of this incredible universe is an infinite loving person who is both
Creator and Redeemer. Even more astounding, this loving
Creator of the galaxies became flesh as an embryo, a growing
baby in the womb of an illiterate virgin living in an oppressed
colony at the edge of the powerful, pagan Roman Empire on a
tiny planet in a small solar system in just one galaxy among the
universe's one hundred-plus billion galaxies.

This baby became a carpenter, then a wandering Jewish
teacher, explaining that the God of the universe cared so much
about the evil ways we mistreat and destroy our neighbors that
God came to live among us both to show us how to love our
neighbors and also to give us the power to do it. Jesus taught us
that the God of the universe is awesome holiness as well as over-
flowing love, and therefore we selfish, sinful persons would have

no hope of standing in the presence of the living God except for one thing—God loves us so much that Jesus takes our sin upon himself and dies in our place so that we can stand unafraid in the presence of infinite holiness.

What makes all of this even more astounding is that this wandering Jewish teacher not only taught an amazing message, but he also made blasphemous claims. The very center of Jewish belief in Jesus' time was that there is only one God. Greek and Roman polytheists believed that gods and goddesses ran around doing strange things, but the Jews knew better. God is one. There is only one God. But the Nazarene Carpenter claimed to have divine authority to forgive sins. At his trial he acknowledged he was the Son of God. When Thomas met the risen Jesus, Thomas uttered the amazing words: "My Lord and my God!" (John 20:28, NIV). This man from Nazareth, the early Christians taught, was also true God, Creator of the galaxies, King of kings and Lord of lords. His bursting from the tomb on the third day, they believed, provided convincing evidence that all his teachings and claims were true.

But Jesus did even more than offer unmerited forgiveness of sins and reveal that he was God in the flesh. He said the long-expected messianic kingdom promised by the prophets of old was actually breaking into history in his person and work. He said the eagerly awaited time of peace and justice was arriving. He taught his disciples to care for the poor, minister to the sick, and love their enemies.

Jesus also challenged the status quo in many ways—the greed of the rich, the neglect and mistreatment of lepers, women, the poor, and the disabled. And Jesus promised that the same almighty God who raised him from the dead would live in his disciples through the Holy Spirit to give them the inner power to live and love the way he did.

Equally astounding, Jesus' earliest disciples taught that God's ultimate plan, at the Second Coming, was to overcome all evil, wickedness, and injustice, and restore to wholeness everything in creation that sin had messed up. They believed that Jesus' ever-growing circle of disciples should and can live now in the knowledge that the decisive victory over evil has already been won and that at Christ's Second Coming, the victory will be completed. In the meantime, you and I are to find meaning and joy as we take our tiny place in this grand cosmic drama. As we share the story of this glorious salvation, inviting others to confess and follow Christ, and as we live like Jesus even now in the midst of a broken world, each one of us plays a tiny but important role in God's grand cosmic drama. As the community of Jesus' disciples truly lives like Jesus, we offer a skeptical, hurting world a little picture of what heaven will be like, a little picture of what the redeemed earth will look like when Christ returns.

I find this story—this true account of God's action in history—utterly dumbfounding. That the Creator of one hundred-plus billion galaxies became flesh on our tiny planet; that our awesomely holy God loves you and me and every other human being so much that God gladly suffered the hell of Roman crucifixion for me, for you, so that whosoever believes in him may be saved; that each one of us is personally invited by the Infinite Lover at the center of the universe not only to live forever in God's presence but even to play a small part now in moving society toward that peace, justice, and wholeness that Christ will perfect at his Second Coming—all that is simply mind-boggling.

I can only bow down in worship and praise.

That, my young friends, is the utterly fantastic Good News that I wanted to review this morning. I say "review," because that in brief is a central part of what you have learned in your four years at Messiah College.

But there is also bad news. What tears my heart out is that so many of the people who claim to embrace this glorious story act as if they do not believe a word of it. The Christian church is supposed to be a little visible picture of what heaven will be like. Instead, so many Christians live just like the world. So many Christians mimic the world rather than follow Jesus. So many Christians commit adultery, worship money, file for divorce, hate their enemies, embrace idolatrous nationalism, and destroy God's creation just like their unbelieving neighbors.

If we had time—and we do not—I could cite reams of polling data and other statistics to underline what I mean.

For now, I'll share just a couple of sad statistics. Polls show that evangelical Christians who claim to have the risen Lord living in their hearts get divorced at about the same rate as the rest of society. In some polls, evangelicals are even more racist than other Americans. One study of a prominent, wonderful evangelical denomination discovered that physical and sexual abuse was just as common in that church as in the rest of society. The Christians living in this country, the richest nation in history, give only about one-fourth of a tithe (2.5 percent of their income) to their churches.[1] If we would just tithe, US Christians could give another $160 billion a year to the work of the kingdom. That $160 billion is more money than all the rich nations of the world give every year to fight poverty and disease in developing countries.

Graduates, in all honesty, I have to say: so many of my generation and your parents' generation of Christians are lukewarm, half-hearted Christians who often have lived more like their sinful neighbors than like Jesus. So I ask you a basic question: Will you be any different? Will you follow Jesus rather than the world?

The awesome God I described stands with arms outstretched pleading with you to live like Jesus. But he will not coerce you. If you want to go to church on Sunday and then worship sex, money, power, and short-term personal self-fulfillment the rest of the week like so many people who call themselves Christians today, God will let you do that, although it breaks God's heart.

But there is a better way. You can decide to live differently from today's lukewarm Christians who mouth Christian words and then mimic the world. You can decide that no matter what the cost, you will live like Jesus. If you do, you will be surprised by joy as God uses you to transform this hurting world.

My friends, small groups of daring pioneers have regularly changed history. Let me remind you of three examples.

About 250 years ago, William Wilberforce was living a self-centered, sinful life as a member of the wealthy British gentry. Then he met Christ in the Wesleyan revival and God transformed his life. For about thirty years, he worked tirelessly as a member of the British Parliament to persuade his nation that slavery was a sin against God and neighbor. It was a hard sell because slavery and the slave trade were major pillars of the British economy. But Wilberforce combined prayer and a passion for evangelism with brilliant political strategy and eventually persuaded the British Parliament to abolish first the slave trade and then slavery itself. This daring evangelical politician changed the course of British history.

Or consider the Student Volunteer Movement. At a conference for university students led by Dwight L. Moody in 1886, a call to evangelize the world in their generation captured the imagination of hundreds of students. Over the next few decades, twenty-five thousand university students became foreign missionaries, tripling the number of Protestant missionaries around the world. The Student Volunteer Movement is one important reason why the number of Christians has grown by leaps and bounds in Africa, Asia, and Latin America in the last one hundred years—transforming the economics, politics, and culture of the planet. A few tens of thousands of committed evangelical university graduates truly changed the world.

Finally, let me tell you about my good friend Wayne Gordon. Wayne grew up in a Christian home in the Midwest. He had perfect Sunday school attendance for several years but had never personally committed his life to Christ. Then, during an Athletes for Christ weekend, when he was in tenth grade, Wayne did that. That Sunday night after returning home, he lay on his bed filled with a new sense of joy. Wayne looked through the ceiling and declared: "Lord, I'll do anything you want me to do with my life."

Almost immediately, he felt a call to the inner city. So Wayne woke up his parents, told them of God's call, and said he must go. Good Christian parents that they were, they said, "That's fine, but you should probably finish high school." Wayne did that—in fact, he graduated from Wheaton College—and then moved into the Lawndale section of West Chicago, one of the twenty poorest neighborhoods in the country at that time.

When Wayne moved into Lawndale, the infant mortality rate there approached the level of very poor countries. Very few students graduated from the failing high schools. It was tough going at first. The night Wayne and his bride returned from their honeymoon, somebody broke into their apartment—and it happened ten more times in the next two years.

Wayne started a Bible club and a recreation club for the youth, and they started to accept Christ. Wayne saw that they needed tutoring, so he started a tutoring program. He saw that they needed health care, so he started a medical center. Today the medical center has dozens of full-time doctors and serves tens of thousands of people every year. The state-of-the-art tutoring program has helped hundreds of youth graduate from college. Wayne's community center has built millions of dollars of low-income housing. The community center is now a tens-of-millions-of-dollars-a-year program transforming a whole neighborhood in Chicago.

At the center of all this work is a church of more than a thousand people—most of whom have come to faith in Christ through the work of the community center. Wayne and all the staff he hires know that people need more than just good health care or job training, although they certainly do need those things. People need Jesus *and* a job. Thousands of people have come to faith in Christ through the work of Wayne's holistic community center.

And all of that started because one young man looked into the face of God and said, "Lord, I'll do anything you want me to do with my life." The result was a life lived in a dramatically different way from that of today's half-hearted Christians.

My young friends, I ask you: Will you be any different from today's lukewarm Christians? Will you make empowering poor people more important than making money? Will you keep your marriage vows even in the hard times? Will you plead at least with the Christians in this hyper-nationalistic country to obey Jesus' command to love our enemies? Will you be business leaders who reject greed? Political leaders who oppose corruption?

The world is waiting for a generation of faithful Christians who will truly live like Jesus.

Our God promises that if you surrender your whole being to God, God will give you the power of the risen Lord to keep your marriage vows and live joyful, lifelong marriages so full of contagious goodness that your neighbors will long to know your Lord. Our God promises to help you give generously, even sacrificially, of your time and money to empower the poor. Our God promises to give you the vision and commitment to restore respect for human life, battle disease, work for peace, and care for creation. The Lord longs to see a new generation of young leaders who will dedicate their lives to sharing the glorious gospel of Jesus with those who have never heard.

There are enough people graduating from Messiah College this morning to transform significant parts of our world in powerful ways. But it all depends on how each of you answers the question: Will you be any different from today's half-hearted Christians?

The Lord stands with arms wide open, inviting you to a life of joyful, costly discipleship. He asks you to surrender every corner of your lives, every hope, every ambition to him.

I beg you, look into his face and promise: I will be different. I will live like you. My Lord, if you give me the strength, I'll do anything you want me to do with my life.

Note

1. See https://nonprofitssource.com/online-giving-statistics/church-giving/.

CHAPTER 17
Biblical Balance, Biblical Balance

> This is my commencement address given at Biblical
> Seminary in Hatfield, Pennsylvania, on June 9, 2018.
> This theme has been central to my thinking, speaking,
> and writing for virtually all of my life.

This is the best of times and the worst of times for evangelical Christians.

Globally, evangelical Christianity, especially the Pentecostal wing, is growing faster than any other part of Christianity. Vast numbers are becoming evangelical Christians in all parts of the Global South—in Africa, Latin America, and Asia.

In the United States over the past fifty years, evangelical Christianity has grown significantly while theologically liberal Christian denominations have declined precipitously.

But there are also devastating problems. Christianity is almost dead in much of Western Europe. And a radical gospel of wealth is widespread in American, African, and Latin American evangelicalism. In the United States, as the sexual revolution starting in the '60s swept across the nation, evangelicals divorced at almost the same rate as the rest of America. Rather than living like Jesus, we conformed to surrounding sinful culture. And today American evangelical youth and vast numbers of global evangelicals are dumbfounded as prominent American evangelical leaders and vast numbers of their followers fail to oppose, or even justify, racism, attacks on immigrants, abuse of women, blatant dishonesty, and idolatrous nationalism. American youth who grew up in evangelical churches are abandoning evangelicalism and some-times even Christian faith in droves. For someone like me who has devoted all his life to trying to help evangelicals follow Jesus more faithfully, it is a time to weep.

But I do not despair. The resurrected Jesus is still Lord. The Bible is still God's unique, authoritative revelation. In fact, a recovery of biblical balance is precisely what we desperately need.

Close to the heart of our problem, close to the tragic failure of evangelicalism, is a one-sided unbiblical understanding of the gospel. Vast segments of popular evangelicalism and some of our theologians seem to think that the gospel is just forgiveness of sins, that Jesus came only to die for our sins so we could go to heaven when we die. My friends, if that is all the gospel is, then it is a one-way ticket to heaven, and we can live like hell until we get there.

But that is simply not what Jesus said his gospel is. In dozens and dozens of places, Jesus clearly said his gospel is the Good News of the kingdom of God. He meant that the long-expected messianic kingdom was actually arriving in his person and work. He was the Messiah and his messianic kingdom was now break-ing into history.

There were clearly two parts to Jesus' dawning kingdom. Jesus told parable after parable, teaching that God is like the father of the prodigal son. God stands with arms outstretched, eager to for-give prodigal sons and daughters who repent. Jesus died on the cross as our substitute. As a result, we broken sinners can stand before a holy God assured of forgiveness through the cross. That is an absolutely wonderful part of Jesus' gospel!

But that is only one-half of Jesus' gospel. The prophets promised that when the Messiah came, there would be not only a new vertical relationship with God but also renewed horizontal right relationships with neighbors. There would be peace and justice in society. Jesus defined his mission in Luke chapter 4, quoting from the prophet Isaiah. Jesus said he came "to proclaim good news to the poor...to

231

proclaim freedom for the prisoners, and recovery of sight for the blind, to set the oppressed free" (v. 18, NIV). And Jesus practiced what he preached. He healed the sick and the blind. When he sent out his disciples, he told them to announce the kingdom and heal the sick. And he warned his followers that if they did not feed the hungry and clothe the naked, they would depart eternally from God.

Jesus' gospel clearly produced a new community of disciples who started to live dramatically differently from surrounding society. Jewish men in Jesus' day often repeated a prayer in which they thanked God they were not Gentiles, slaves, or women. In Jesus' new community of the early church, Paul could declare confidently that there was neither Jew or Gentile, slave or free, rich or poor, male or female because they were all one in Christ (Galatians 3:28). Central to their understanding of Jesus' gospel of the kingdom was the fact that it demanded new socioeconomic relationships in the body of Christ. That meant that the worst racial hatred in the ancient world was being overcome as Jews accepted Gentiles as brothers and sisters. That meant that the rich shared dramatically with the poor. That meant that men accepted women as equals in Christ's new kingdom. These new socioeconomic relationships in the body of Christ are just as much a part of the gospel as forgiveness of sins.

In both testaments and throughout history, we see God's people trying to separate their relationship with God from their relationship with people. We would like to be accepted with God without that affecting how we treat our neighbor. If Jesus' gospel were just forgiveness of sins, that would work. We could get saved and still go on being racist, sexist, and unconcerned about the poor. And that is what so much of evangelicalism has done and still does. The blatant moral failure of so much of American evangelicalism results to a significant degree from this failure to see that Jesus' gospel includes both forgiveness of sins and the call to be Jesus' new socioeconomic community rejecting racism, sexism, idolatrous nationalism, and hatred of enemies.

Our one-sided gospel is actually heresy. Heresy is never a total denial of revealed truth. Rather, it is a one-sided embrace of part of the truth in a way that ignores another important part. That is what popular evangelicalism has done by defining the gospel as only forgiveness of sins rather than the gospel of the kingdom. I think that one-sided, heretical gospel is a central cause of the cheap grace so widespread in the evangelical church. If evangelicals are to follow Jesus rather than the world in the area of divorce; if we are to follow Jesus rather than the world in our racial attitudes, economic practices, attitudes about truth and treatment of women, then we must recover Jesus' gospel of the kingdom. We must embrace both the vertical and horizontal aspects of Jesus' gospel. We must recover the biblical balance that emphasizes both that Jesus' gospel includes the wonderful reality that God forgives sinners and that Jesus' kingdom community is to be a new, visible society now living in faithfulness to all Jesus taught. Biblical balance is what we need.

But biblical balance is important in every area, not just our understanding of Jesus' gospel. Biblical balance is important in our personal lives as we seek to combine prayer and action. It is central to the life of the local congregation as it combines the inward journey of worship, fellowship, and nurture with the outward journey of mission to the world. It is crucial as we seek a proper balance of evangelism and social concern in our practice of mission. And it is essential as we seek to shape political life in a way that is faithful to Christ.

Let's look at each of those points briefly. First prayer and action. I am an activist by natural instinct. My first impulse, when I see a problem, is to write an article or call a meeting or form a committee and strategize about what actions would be wise and effective. I don't think that strategizing and acting are bad. God gave us brains to use. And if we simply talk about problems and fail to do something about them, we are hypocritical phonies and unfaithful disciples. But surely our first move, when we sense a problem, should be to pray and seek the guidance of the Holy Spirit. Just as surely, all of our strategizing and acting should be immersed in prayer. If Jesus needed to stop preaching and healing to spend time in prayer, then surely we need to do the same. In our activist-oriented society, Christians desperately need to recover a biblical balance of prayer and action.

Second, we need biblical balance in the local congregation. By all means, we need vibrant worship, warm fellowship, and challenging nurture of each other within the local congregation. But so many of our congregations are largely self-centered. They spend almost all their money and time on the inner life of the congregation. But mission to the world is also central to biblical faith. Jesus' last command was to go everywhere, leading people to Christ and teaching them to obey all that he had taught. Would it not be more faithful to Jesus if the typical congregation spent 50 percent of its budget on the internal life of the congregation and 50 percent on mission outside the congregation? I pray that you, as future pastors and leaders, will dare to call your people to a biblical balance of inner congregational life and outward mission to the world.

Third, we need biblical balance in the way we embrace both evangelism and social action. For a great part of the twentieth century, some churches focused almost exclusively on evangelism and other churches almost entirely on social action. Fortunately, the evangelical world has made major progress in the last forty years in embracing both. In 1973 the Chicago Declaration of Evangelical Social Concern called evangelicals to greater engagement with societal issues such as racism, economic justice, oppression of women, and violent nationalism. In 1974 the Lausanne Covenant declared boldly that evangelism and social responsibility are both part of our Christian duty. And in the following years, more and more evangelical leaders and congregations began to combine evangelistic outreach with programs that ministered to the social needs of people. Evangelical relief and development agencies flourished. John Perkins developed a powerful model of effective holistic ministry to urban and rural poor that led thousands to Christ and also provided better education, health care, job training, and housing for needy people. Today most young evangelicals just assume that faithful Christians combine word and deed.

But it is very easy to lose the balance. Again and again, Christian ministries like the YMCA started out with a great combination of evangelism and social action. And then they slowly lost the evangelism. In my lifetime, I have known younger evangelical social activists who became so upset by the failure of evangelical leaders to deal with things like racism and economic injustice that they abandoned any concern for evangelism. I sometimes worry about younger evangelicals today. They say they just assume that faithful Christians embrace both word and deed. But in practice they actually spend most of their time and money on social action. A few years ago, I wrote an article for *Relevant* magazine, whose readers are almost entirely younger Christians. I praised them for their passion for social justice, but I also begged them not to forget evangelism.

Jesus is our only perfect model. Jesus preached and healed. Jesus did not think he should spend all his time preaching. The Gospels show that Jesus spent a lot of potential preaching time ministering to the physical needs of people. But just as certainly, Jesus did not spend all his time caring for people's physical needs. We must strive to live like Jesus in mission. I urge and beg you as future pastors to pray for, teach, and live out a biblical balance of evangelism and social action in your congregations.

Finally, we desperately need biblical balance in our political activity as evangelicals. I know this is a complicated, sensitive topic. I will not tell you how to vote this November. But I would think that one of the first things evangelicals should ask when they think about faithful political engagement is this: "What does the Bible tells us that

God cares about?" When one asks that question, it becomes clear that God cares about both the sanctity of human life and racial justice; about both marriage and justice for the poor; about both sexual integrity and care for creation. The official public policy document of the National Association of Evangelicals states that "faithful evangelical civic engagement must champion a biblically balanced agenda" (https://www.forthehealth.net/method-christian-civic-engagement). And the document goes on to make strong statements on the sanctity of human life and marriage between a man and a woman. But it also has vigorous sections on the importance of economic justice, care for creation, and opposing racism.

A few decades ago, there was a prominent pro-life senator who was nationally known as a champion for opposing abortion. But he was from the largest tobacco-growing state, so he defended government subsidies for tobacco-growers. He even promoted using our tax dollars to ship American tobacco to poor countries under our Food for Peace program! That was not exactly a consistently pro-life stance! Some wag has suggested that some pro-life people act as if life begins at conception and ends at birth. But if one is completely pro-life (as I seek to be), then one must defend the sanctity of human life wherever it is threatened. Preventing people from dying of starvation and addressing inadequate health care are also pro-life issues.

When evangelical Christians are supportive of political movements that fail to condemn, or even encourage, racism; that neglect economic justice for all, especially the poor; and that fail to care for the environment the Creator has given us, they abandon a biblical balance and discredit Christian faith. Truth-telling is as essential to following Jesus as it is to a vibrant democracy. Evangelicals who remember Jesus' words that the truth will set us free should be the strongest advocates of truth in public life.

It is always difficult to embrace a fully biblical balance in one's political decisions. Regularly, one politician or party will be closer to a biblically defined agenda on some issues and the other person and party will be closer on other issues. I acknowledge that political choices in this nation at this time are extremely difficult. But biblically committed evangelicals ought to be widely known as the strongest advocates for both the sanctity of human life and economic justice; for both supporting marriage and rejecting racism; for both sexual integrity and care for creation and truth-telling. Biblical balance is what evangelical political voices should promote. That is what the public should think of when they think of evangelical political engagement.

So, to you graduates today I say this: As you become pastors and leaders in church and society, please beg the Lord to help you embrace and promote a biblical balance. Embrace both the vertical and horizontal parts of Jesus' gospel. Everywhere share with broken people the glorious news that no matter how badly they have messed up, God stands with wide-open arms, eager to forgive their sins. Then, with equal vigor, teach all who confess Christ to live like Jesus now so that the church is a little picture of what the completed kingdom will be like when Christ returns.

I urge you to preach, teach, and live the biblical balance of prayer and action. Nurture congregations that every year lead scores of people to confess Christ for the first time, and then throw their arms around the poor, broken people in society and walk with them toward wholeness. And finally, as pastors, do not tell your people how to vote. But dare to help your people embrace a biblically balanced political agenda in their civic engagement so that when the world speaks of evangelical political activity, they say, "Those evangelicals are the leaders in protecting the sanctity of human life and marriage. And they are also the leaders in rejecting racism, empowering the poor, protecting the environment, and telling the truth."

My friends, I urge you: make biblical balance your guiding star.

CHAPTER 18

A Morning Prayer

I often fail to come even close to the submission and
faithfulness prayed for here, but it represents my desire.
I am fairly certain I wrote this prayer decades ago,
although I do not know when. And if I actually found
it and forgot the author, I apologize.

Father, in the morning of this new day, I joyfully and grateful-
ly submit every fiber of my being to you and your will. I surrender every corner of my life, every ounce of personal ambition, striving, and longing to you and your kingdom. By your
grace, I ask for that purity of heart that wills only one thing—
your will and glory.

Lord Jesus, in the morning of this new day, I ask for the grace
to make every decision and perform every single act according to
the values of your kingdom, according to the model you lived
and taught.

And, blessed Holy Spirit, in the morning of this new day, I
implore you to shower upon me the fullness of your fruits, gifts,
and power. Please intercede for me with groans too deep for
human utterance so that all this day I may live and act for the
honor and glory of the God whom I love and adore, Father, Son,
and Holy Spirit. Amen.